Laura Huang is an associate professor at Harvard Business School; previously, she was an assistant professor at the Wharton School, University of Pennsylvania. Her research has been featured in the *New York Times*, the *Financial Times*, the *Wall Street Journal*, *USA Today*, *Forbes* and *Nature*. Her research has won numerous awards including a 2016 Kauffman Foundation Fellowship. Huang was named one of the 40 Best Business School Professors Under the Age of 40 by Poets & Quants. *Edge* is her first book.

Praise for *Edge*

'We're all looking for an edge. But where does it come from? In this insightful and accessible book, Laura Huang provides the answers. Be authentic and distinct. Provide value to others. And turn adversity into advantage. Packed with fascinating stories and counterintuitive principles, *Edge* is a must-read for anyone seeking to stand out from the crowd'
　　　　— Daniel H. Pink, author of *When*, *Drive* and *To Sell Is Human*

'This book will change how you navigate your career and overcome obstacles along the way. Do yourself, and those you work with, a favour and read it now!'
　　　　— Marie Forleo, author of *Everything is Figureoutable* and founder of B-School

'*Edge* is for anyone who has found themselves feeling underestimated and unequipped to deal with a tough situation – so, all of us. Huang melds her ground-breaking research with heartfelt stories to show how all of us can – and indeed, must – create our own advantage'
　　　　— Arlan Hamilton, founder and managing partner of Backstage Capital

'*Edge* is fun to read, beautifully written and resonant – a worthy addition to every entrepreneur's toolbox. Laura Huang is a powerful new voice for those that seek to make a ruckus'
　　　　— Seth Godin, author of *This Is Marketing*

'When hard work alone isn't enough, what do you do? *Edge* is an invaluable guide to decoding the biases and harmful perceptions about you and your work that might be standing in your way. Huang masterfully weaves together original research and powerful stories that will leave you newly inspired and empowered to take charge of your biggest challenges'
　　　　— Susan David, Harvard Medical School psychologist, author of *Emotional Agility*

'*Edge* is a superbly researched, deeply insightful and persuasive book that is destined to be a guidebook for self-empowerment and success. It's truly out of this world'
　　　　— Terry Virts, former NASA astronaut, International Space Station Commander, US Air Force Fighter Pilot

'Laura Huang's research on bias and gut feeling has moved the field forward significantly. Not only is she an incredible researcher, she has written a compelling, crucial book that will help readers take control of their toughest challenges with poise and authenticity'
　　　　— Seth Stephens-Davidowitz, *New York Times*-bestselling author of *Everybody Lies*

Edge

Turning Adversity into Advantage

LAURA HUANG

piatkus

PIATKUS

First published in the US in 2020 by Portfolio, an imprint of Penguin Random House LLC
First published in Great Britain in 2020 by Piatkus

1 3 5 7 9 10 8 6 4 2

A CIP catalogue record for this book
is available from the British Library.

ISBN 978-0-349-42227-5

Typeset in Minion by M Rules
Printed and bound in Great Britain by Clays Ltd, Elcograf SpA

Papers used by Piatkus are from well-managed forests and
other responsible sources.

Piatkus
An imprint of
Little, Brown Book Group
Carmelite House
50 Victoria Embankment
London EC4Y 0DZ

An Hachette UK Company
www.hachette.co.uk

www.improvementzone.co.uk

For A and L

CONTENTS

Edge

A COLLEAGUE RECENTLY TOLD ME ABOUT A PERSON WHO HAD managed to get a face-to-face meeting with Elon Musk, the entrepreneur famous for founding Tesla and SpaceX. Getting a meeting is not an easy feat. This is a man who once told his alma mater (the Wharton School of the University of Pennsylvania) not to call him more than once a year, and that even then, the answer is probably no. Musk's net worth is around $20.2 billion, so each minute of his time is worth thousands of dollars, even calculated conservatively.

But the reason this story is noteworthy is not because an unknown, unimportant individual was able to get a meeting with him in the first place. It's because Elon ended the meeting not more than thirty seconds later. As the story goes, he took one look at his visitor and said, "No. Get out of my office."

It shows how difficult it is to actually get access to someone of that stature. (And how even if you do, it doesn't ensure that you'll be heard.) It emphasizes how the rich and powerful must be blunt and maintain unyielding focus on what furthers their own careers. It demonstrates that the time and resources of someone like Musk are so well protected that access—let alone any gains that might result—is near impossible.

As this person finished telling the story to me, he commented, "Anyway, I don't know if this story is even actually true."

To which I replied, "It's true." And I know it's true because the person who got kicked out of Elon Musk's office was me.

· · ·

The meeting with Elon happened serendipitously. A friend of mine was in the audience when Elon was giving a university commencement speech and lucked his way into getting the billionaire's contact info. And that was how this friend of mine, Byron (who generously invited me along), and I found ourselves waiting for our appointment with Elon, sitting in his SpaceX office.

Byron knew I was working on research that examined the challenges that start-up companies in the private space industry face as they go up against massive players such as Boeing, Lockheed Martin, and even the US government and NASA. We planned to talk to Elon about his thoughts on the future of private space tourism—the opportunity for normal people ("normal" meaning those who have two hundred thousand dollars to spend on a trip aboard a space shuttle) to take a suborbital flight to experience three to six minutes of weightlessness, a view of a twinkle-free star field, and a vista of the curved earth below.

Knowing how special this opportunity was, Byron and I had prepared well. We had put lots of hard work and effort into our research. We knew an immense amount about SpaceX and the private space industry. We knew Elon's entire life history. We had a list of well-researched, intelligent questions on hand. We had specific topics in mind, an understanding of any current events he could have mentioned, and thoughtful perspectives on all aspects of his business (not just SpaceX but also Tesla, PayPal, and even Hyperloop). We even had some ideas for how we could help his companies, and we had a small gift for him. We were prepared.

Except that none of our hard work was going to make much of a difference. Because as I alluded to earlier, we got kicked out of his office (which was really just his cubicle in the corner of an open office floor plan, in case anyone was interested).

Almost. That's where the story got it wrong. Elon did *try* to kick us out of his office. But somehow we were able to regain our composure and turn what was quite nearly a thirty-second disaster into an invigorating hour-long conversation.

. . .

It's true that the first word he said to us was *no*. Literally, we sat down, he looked at us, and he said, "No." I was totally disoriented, and looked at him blankly and asked, "No?" To which he replied, "No." And then he told us to leave.

Somehow during this rather disorienting "oh shit" moment, I suddenly realized that his eyes weren't, in fact, on us. They were on something Byron was holding: the gift that we had brought him.

I realized that Elon didn't know we were academics. He thought we were entrepreneurs trying to pitch him and that the gift was a product prototype. He thought we wanted something from him: his endorsement, or his money, or some sort of support for the company that we were presumably starting. Of course he said no. This is a man who is *constantly* getting asked for things and constantly barraged with requests. His default response has to be no. Even when the requests come from completely legitimate and powerful people—but especially when they come from two young and seemingly unimportant people.

And so it was that this meeting almost ended disastrously—except that I did something out of the blue that somehow humored him beyond belief.

It was nothing special. It certainly wasn't premeditated. I just started giggling. Maybe I should have simply nodded politely and left, but the giggling gave Elon pause. I sputtered through my uncontrollable laughter: "You thinking we're pitching you? [more uncontrollable laughter] We don't want your money. . . . What, like you're rich or something?"

That threw him off completely, and then he started laughing uncontrollably.* He realized that we didn't want anything from him (or at least not his money or endorsement for our "product"), and we endeared ourselves enough to him to at least not get kicked out of the meeting.

Truth be told, we crushed the meeting. We chatted, debated, riffed, and by the end, we were like old friends (okay, not really, but he did give me a hug on the way out).

And upon leaving, Elon gave us a card with the contact details of someone who headed up operations for SpaceX. He told us that he could help us obtain more information about what we were studying. In the end, he offered up exactly the kind of resources and connections that he thought we had initially wanted.

Why were we able to turn it around and endear ourselves to him?

We gained an edge. We gained an edge over one of the richest, most powerful men in the country.

---

* I have no idea why he found me so funny, but there is research on mimicking, which suggests that in situations of uncertainty, people mirror your behaviors and actions, so there's that.

• • •

What do I mean by "edge"? Having an edge is about gaining an advantage, but it goes beyond just advantage. It's about recognizing that others will have their own perceptions about us, right or wrong. When you recognize the power in those perceptions and learn to use them in your favor, you create an edge.

Certain people seem to be endowed with a unique advantage in which they can execute faster and better and get the things they need, because they are positioned in such a way that others help them move forward. These people have a well-oiled path to success, something that just makes success and achievement flow more easily. It is like rowing with the current carrying you.

In some circumstances, this might be you. But in *many* circumstances—those that are nonetheless important and critical—it's not.

Gaining an edge is about knowing that even without certain endowments, you can *create* an advantage for yourself, especially in the circumstances that are most challenging and consequential.

Let me say more.

People generally underestimate two things:

1. How hard it is to get your foot in the door as an outsider (whatever "outsider" means to you).

2. How wide doors are open once you're on the inside.

That is what this book is about. You can create your own edge and open doors—wide-open doors—for yourself.

Gaining an edge is critical in nearly all situations. Sometimes, it's about taking charge of tough challenges in the moment, such as in pitch meetings, job interviews, or public presentations. But it's also about furthering your career strategically over the long term. Structural inequity and bias are real, and we must acknowledge that they play a significant part in whether people will be successful. This book is about going beyond those whom we see as typically having an advantage, and how having an *edge* transcends gender, race, ethnicity, age, and wealth, so that you can thrive and flourish regardless of these factors. We will all find ourselves at a disadvantage from time to time. Creating an edge means that we give ourselves the ability to turn those disadvantages into unique assets—to turn adversity into an advantage.

• • •

Over the course of my career, I've studied those who have been *underestimated* and *disadvantaged*—entrepreneurs who can't get funding for their ventures, employees who are never able to rise to higher levels in an organization, medical patients who die in emergency rooms because of unequal treatment. I've studied how we make perceptions and attributions about people's character and competence as a result. I've studied how "soft" factors*—such as personality, the extent to which you are seen as trustworthy, passionate, or committed, and the way you interact with people—rather than objective data, drive the decisions and outcomes of individuals and firms. My work has helped me understand my own journey—from a child of immigrants with humble beginnings, to years of being underestimated and facing obstacles, constraints, and setbacks, to where I am now, a Harvard

---

* I've petitioned at times to rename "soft skills" as "core skills" or even "power skills" for this very reason. You can't really be successful without them.

professor who is privileged enough to have the chance to share what I've learned about how individuals can create their own edge.

I draw from my own personal experiences, sharing what went through my head as I faced those who underestimated me. I've also sought out individuals, teams, and companies—some who have always naturally seemed to have an edge, some who have had to create an edge, and some who gained an edge and lost it. I share their stories, and mine, because I have seen the power of those who are able to take the perceptions, attributions, and stereotypes of others—the very things that were meant to personally disadvantage them—and turn them around to work in their favor. These are people and companies who have turned adversity into advantage, obstacles into opportunities, and bias into breaks. Alongside these stories, I'll illuminate relevant sociological, psychological, and business research and theories.

This book is *not* about "gaming the system" or relying on insincere methods; there is no magic formula offering you instant success. Instead, I show how you can harness your personality and strengths—and even your weaknesses—to create a unique edge. The more of yourself you put into creating this edge, the more powerful it becomes—an advantage that could only be yours.

And that's the key, because not only will you know yourself more intimately, you will also have the tools to influence how others value and understand you. Those who are able to create the most effective and most sustained edge are the ones who are actually the most sincere, because their edge comes from a place of authenticity and self-knowledge.

Regardless of whether it appears to be through a thoughtful, premeditated process or a spontaneous natural reaction, you can effectively influence external circumstances in your favor—like we did with Elon.

Because we were able to spontaneously delight Elon, a door opened for us to guide his perceptions away from seeing us as entrepreneurs asking for money. He could then perceive us in a way that we intended, rather than based on his own quick judgments and stereotypes. In turn, we showed him how we brought value to the discussion and how engaging with us actually enriched his own perspective. Those who can create that for themselves are the ones who *Enrich*, *Delight*, and *Guide*—to make their *Effort* go further. These four concepts make up the core structure of this book.

The first part of this book is called "<u>E</u>nrich." The foundation of your edge is your ability to provide value to and enrich those around you. This section focuses on the difference between those who truly enrich and bring value to others and those who don't actually bring value (but are good at convincing others that they do). Those who have an edge are the former; they *do* bring value, rather than posturing about the supposed value they bring (we all know people like that). Those who have an edge, however, are also able to demonstrate and effectively communicate the value they bring, rather than leaving it up to others to guess.

I'll share some of the ways to identify how to enrich in a way that creates an edge, and the tools that you have at your disposal to both identify and communicate the value you bring. I'll challenge you to reflect on why we see constraints as impediments, sharing stories about how to flip them into opportunities. Along the way, you'll discover the significance of self-knowledge, which provides an inimitable type of worth: with an eye on your true assets *and* shortcomings, you can create your own unique advantages.

The second part of the book is called "<u>D</u>elight." Before you can enrich, you have to be let in. Byron and I knew how we could enrich Elon's businesses—but he didn't. We had to delight him first in order to gain the opportunity to show him how we could add value. Those who already have an understanding of how they enrich are most equipped to delight. I'll show what delighting another person means, and why it is so important. You'll see how delighting isn't synonymous with being charming or entertaining, or charismatic in the typical sense. Everyone has the power to delight, as you'll learn from the story of a woman who was laid off from her job, only to find them begging her to stay. You'll see how delight can help pacify skepticism and misgivings, how the director of a famous movie was able to convince an even more famous band to set aside stereotypes so that they could together rewrite the narrative on biases and prejudices, and how a father was able to change his young daughter's view of what it meant to be an empowered, emboldened individual so that she too could have an edge.

The third part of the book is called "Guide." Gaining an edge is about you in relation to other people. It's about navigating the perceptions we have of ourselves, the perceptions others have of us, and the attributions about our skills, competence, and character that are made as a result. This section explains how we can empower ourselves to guide our own contexts.

When we know (and can figure out) how others see us, it gives us the capacity to guide and redirect that perception, so that we can influence how they grasp and appreciate the value we command and the edge we bring. You'll see how this paved the way for one woman's journey from bookkeeper to Louis Vuitton executive, and how an entrepreneur scored a massive funding check despite initially being disparaged for his foreign accent. From there, I'll consider why it is that when we more fully own what is within us, by making allowances for what is around us, we actually end up affecting others more organically and authentically, furthering the edge that we have.

I'll close with the final part, "Effort," in which I'll point to how effort and hard work reinforce the edge that you create for yourself. Sometimes it's as much what we *do* as it is the effort that we put into *not* doing other things. Don't be mistaken—hard work is critical. But ultimately, gaining an edge requires hard work, *plus*. You need hard work, but when so many decisions are driven by the outside perceptions of others, you also need to know how to allocate effort.

When you learn to identify what these perceptions are, how they operate, and the attributions that people are making about your character and abilities, you can empower yourself to face challenges with grace and to smooth your path to success. You give yourself the ability to delight others, open up opportunities, and strategically guide the interactions that you have with others. In short: you create an edge.

A final note: When I was first approached to write this book, I was extremely hesitant. I didn't want to write something that was going to be just like the books that other business school professors have written. I pointed out that I wouldn't be able to give examples of prominent, well-known people and how they gained an edge. I wouldn't be able to present idealized stories about people we know, such as Thomas Edison,* Elvis Presley, Bruce Lee, Margaret Thatcher, W. E. B. Du Bois, and Frida Kahlo. I'd instead be telling stories about Oussama, a nondescript French-Lebanese man who so charmed me with his story that I ended up telling my husband to apply to work at the company that Oussama later started. For every story I'd be telling about someone like the Olympic medal–winning figure skater Mirai Nagasu, I'd be sharing twice that number of examples of people like Oussama, or my

---

* Who, incidentally, was actually a ruthless businessman who stole ideas from people and claimed them as his own, I discovered.

neighborhood hairdresser, Jennie, or Peter, a student of mine looking for an internship.

But it is precisely *because* I can share the stories of ordinary people who didn't have their foot in the door that I finally agreed to write this book. My hope is that through the experiences of normal, otherwise unexceptional individuals like you and me, you'll see how they were able to create an edge despite their seeming disadvantage. I hope that you'll see the power and potential of creating *your* edge, in instances where *you* are underestimated, just as I have learned from my years of research on disadvantage. And I hope the research and stories in this book will show you what works, but just as important, what doesn't work.

CHAPTER 1

Hard Work, *Plus*

Sometimes success is disguised as hard work.

—S. Truett Cathy

IN 2018, MIRAI NAGASU BECAME THE FIRST AMERICAN WOMAN TO land a triple axel at the Olympics. How did she do it? Hard work and perseverance, of course.

Before she ever set foot on an ice rink, Nagasu spent most of her childhood in a storage room at the sushi restaurant that her parents owned in suburban Los Angeles. They couldn't afford a babysitter for her, so while they worked, Nagasu would do homework on her own and then sleep on a yoga mat until closing time. It is there, she maintains, that she picked up these important life skills of hard work and perseverance. "I have a great work ethic because I've watched my parents work super hard," Nagasu once said. She often speaks about how her father, Kiyoto, refused to take vacations, rarely taking time off because closing the restaurant would mean his employees would go without pay. In fact, the very evening that she performed her historic triple axel, her parents were working the dinner rush at their restaurant.

With this type of work ethic and drive, it's no wonder her Olympic teammates, such as Vincent Zhou, who made Olympics history by landing the first quadruple lutz, have described Nagasu as "the hardest worker I know."

Nagasu's story exemplifies a core belief: those who work hard and put in the effort will be rewarded. We teach our children this from day one, and even double down on this advice as they inevitably face challenges and disappointments, reemphasizing that hard work is the ticket to success.

Yes, you may experience hardship and failure, but with even more hard work, effort, and perseverance, you will overcome. We've all heard some version of this. It is a message that is universally ingrained in us, a phenomenon that transcends cultures. "Rome wasn't built in a day, but they were laying bricks every hour." "A winner is a loser who tried one more time."* "The most certain way to succeed is to just try one more time."

In my family, growing up, it was always the story about how my mother immigrated to the United States from Taiwan with just twenty-two dollars in her pocket. Through sheer hard work and perseverance, she was able to provide everything that my brother and I ever needed, even after she lost my father and became a single mother.

Lots of us have some version of this family story. It's also reiterated in the books we read and the movies we watch. Like Daniel-san in *The Karate Kid*,† a bullied teen who learned self-defense from Mr. Miyagi,

---

* Although honestly, sometimes this just makes me feel like a loser.
† The original, 1984 version—the only version as far as I'm concerned.

an elderly gardener who also was a karate master. With hard work and perseverance, not only does Daniel defeat his nemesis in the final tournament, he also gets the girl. Or *Braveheart*,* anyone? The story of a man who sets out to avenge the deaths of his relatives and his secret bride, taking on the might of a ruling powerhouse to become a symbol of freedom for his country. There's a reason it grossed $210.4 million in worldwide sales and won five Academy Awards including Best Picture, Best Director, and Best Cinematography—it's an extremely powerful story that gives us hope and the push to fight our battles.

It's a deep-rooted sentiment that also transcends cultural boundaries. It's stories like Gac Filipaj's, an Albanian refugee who was a school janitor for almost two decades, mopping floors and emptying garbage cans. Despite the exhausting work and his low pay, he put aside both money and energy for one or two classes each semester. At the age of fifty-two, he received his degree, graduating with honors.

It's stories like Sanghoon's, who was raised on a small farm in a tiny village. He had to walk four miles to attend a one-room school, but through sheer hard work and determination ended up attending Sungkyunkwan University, one of the most prestigious universities in Seoul, South Korea, and becoming a nuclear physicist.

At a time when issues of social class are front and center, stories like these send a reminder that though class distinctions exist,† social

---

* I also love *Slumdog Millionaire* (2009), in which a chaiwala (tea person), an illiterate orphan from the slums of India, is on the verge of winning the ultimate prize on a popular TV quiz show.
† In fact, in some countries, there are separate classes identified beyond the typical middle-, upper-, and working-class designations; for example, in the UK, there are seven distinct classes.

mobility is possible. Your background does not limit how well you can expect to do in life—if you earn it.

But the reality rarely plays out that way. What if we think back to Mirai Nagasu and what *actually* happened? Well, before her triumphant triple axel at the 2018 Olympics, she was unceremoniously shut out of the 2014 Olympics figure skating team. She placed third at the national championships, which should have landed her one of the three spots on the Olympic team. Instead, the United States Figure Skating Association chose to give that spot to Ashley Wagner, who had placed fourth at the championship, by exercising their power of discretion and deeming Wagner a better bet than Nagasu.

This kind of substitution from the skating federation was unprecedented. One of the reasons they cited for making this decision? Nagasu was only twenty, and Wagner, at twenty-three, was more mature and experienced. Yet Polina Edmunds, who placed a surprise second in 2014, right in front of Nagasu, was only fifteen years old and had less experience than Nagasu.

Perhaps that is why US Figure Skating chose against Nagasu. Or, more dismally, perhaps it was because Nagasu wasn't the picture-perfect image of an American ice skater—blond and fair skinned—as the three selected skaters were.* The federation denied racial bias, but decisions can sometimes speak louder than denials.

So what happens when hard work doesn't work?

. . .

We are all trying to get ahead in our careers, goals, and ambitions. Sometimes it's about making it to the Olympics. Sometimes it's about

---

* Gracie Gold was the third American woman selected for the team; she placed first in the national championships.

making an impact or creating change; other times it's about getting that promotion or getting funding for your new company. No matter the goal, the secret to success, we are told, is working hard. Hard work will speak for itself.

But something in the back of our minds tells us that this is not the entire story. That you can take two people who both work extremely hard—even put in the exact same amount of hard work—and one will be more successful and the other will fall short. Or, as Nagasu's story shows, we can even perform better than our competitors and still get shut out.

We've all been burned before. We've all had experiences in which we worked hard, delivered the best product, and still ended up losing out. What we implicitly realize, when we admit it, is that success is actually rarely about meritocracy—the quality of your idea, the amount of effort you put in, the objective skills you have. Those who get access to the critical ingredients for success—vital resources and the money, time, and advice of others to help us achieve our goals—are not always the ones with the best credentials or ideas.

· · ·

A few years ago, I was a volunteer mentor in a program that matched at-risk youth just starting high school with mentors who were fairly established in their careers. One of the things we got to do was spend their entire first week of school with them, with the goal of helping them adjust to a new environment and helping them get off to a great start. My "little sister," Cerelina, was a bright, spunky thirteen-year-old, and I was quickly besotted by her. I accompanied her to her first class, a freshman history class, and quietly sat in the back, after giving her a fist pump of encouragement.

Because it was the first day of school, I watched as her history teacher went through the normal rules of the class and gave a brief overview of what they would be covering that year. And then, toward the end of the class, he gave each student an index card and asked them to write down a goal, something that they were striving to achieve by the end of high school. He gave the students a few minutes and then collected them. Then, he went through and read them out loud to the class, one by one. They had been instructed to put their names on their cards, but he didn't read whose card was whose (thank goodness).

The cards listed ideas like "My goal is to make the football team," "I want to beat my brother at *Mario Kart*," and "My goal is to save up enough money for Steph Currys" (a type of shoe, apparently). And there was one from a wisecracking kid who was immediately popular and seemed to be instantaneously adored by everyone; he raised his hand and confidently acknowledged, "That one's mine," when the teacher read out, "My goal is to teach everyone in this class how to spell Zimbabwe."

So the history teacher was going through these cards and reading them out loud, and commenting after each one. "Yup, you've got a great football arm—I think you'll make it," "Steph Currys? What happened to Air Jordans?" and even "Zimbabwe . . . I'll make sure you all know how that country is spelled, *and* where it is!"

And then the teacher read a card that said, "My goal for high school is to study hard and be awarded a Rhodes Scholarship to study at Oxford University." I immediately knew who it belonged to—earlier, Cerelina had told me about a book she had just finished reading about a girl who got a Rhodes Scholarship to Oxford, and asked me where Oxford was. My heart swelled with pride.

As the teacher read Cerelina's card, I noticed he was smirking, and then I heard him chuckle and comment, "Ambitious," and then under his breath, "Let's not get our hopes up." I remember glancing over at Cerelina, her face burning with embarrassment.

I pulled her aside after class and told her Oxford was a wonderful goal—that she could do it, and that with hard work and perseverance, nothing could stop her. But years later, despite her hard work (and my constant encouragement about the power of hard work), she fell far short, getting pregnant and dropping out of high school.

And the part that will always haunt me? On the day she dropped out, after apologizing for disappointing me—which she hadn't—she brought up that index card from her first day of high school. She told me, "I should have just written that I wanted to make the cheerleading squad.* Hard work doesn't get people like me into Oxford. Hard work doesn't work that way for me."

We don't need to be reminded about hard work and effort. We already know. But what we don't know as much about is how to navigate the nuanced nature of the disadvantages we all will face at some point in time—and how to build the capacity to cultivate the skills and tools that will allow us to take control and create a new starting position for ourselves. Create circumstances in which hard work *does* reap the benefits, rewards, and success. "Life is not a matter of holding good cards, but of playing a poor hand well," Robert Louis Stevenson once said. That's what you get with an edge.

---

* And for the record, I am not suggesting any undertones here about cheerleaders at all. In fact, I was a cheerleader in high school.

It's Not Just About Bias

Cerelina and Mirai both faced adversity in terms of how others perceived them, to say the least. Cerelina's teacher saw her dreams as too ambitious for someone like her, a girl from a low-income neighborhood. The US Figure Skating Association's choice suggested to some ageist and racist decision making.

But harmful perceptions such as these can actually be a key to overcoming adversity. If creating an edge is the antidote, perceptions are the poison—but also part of the cure. We are cognitively limited creatures who must rely on our perceptions to help us organize and make sense of those we encounter in the world. We haven't evolved past the fight-or-flight responses that helped our ancient ancestors grapple with dangers in their environment, and this has resulted in biases and disadvantages. Sometimes, our perceptions lead to explicit partiality and bias, like when a hiring manager openly decides not to hire older candidates because of the perception that they don't understand technology.

Other times, we aren't even consciously aware of bias—for instance, when we hire the taller candidate. Research demonstrates that many of us implicitly believe that taller people are smarter, better leaders, and ultimately more successful in life. In fact, while only 15 percent of the total population is over six feet tall, 58 percent of CEOs in the United States are; only 4 percent of the general population is taller than six feet two, but nearly 33 percent of CEOs are six feet two or taller. My colleagues and I have even found that something as basic as someone's attractiveness can give people—especially males—an extra boost in positive perceptions.

In my own research, I have found that patient-provider interactions and treatment decisions are impacted by which patients are deemed to have the highest pain threshold (spoiler alert: women are assumed to be able to handle more pain). In fact, my inimitable, brilliant coauthors, Brad Greenwood and Seth Carnahan, and I found that implicit perceptions of patients are so considerable and matter so much that women were less likely to survive emergency heart attacks when treated by a male physician. Perceptions can literally impact life-or-death outcomes.*

But perceptions are not just about gender—or race or ethnicity or any of the standard characters that come to mind when we think about bias. Put simply, no one is immune. It is not a competitive hierarchy of who has it worse. Disadvantage is situational. I've seen males, for example, face egregious bias. Not too long ago, a school district in Philadelphia was found to be hiring female teachers at much higher pay levels than their male counterparts, and further, was giving them more credit for their prior teaching experience. But what was perhaps even worse was that these male teachers, during their interviews, were getting asked questions like "Why do you even want to work with kids? I always wonder why any healthy male would want to work with kids," and "I just want to make sure that you're not a pervert."

It is important to note that bias is not just about the disadvantaged minority. It is pervasive and takes on many different forms. It's easy to label someone as a "privileged rich kid." It's harder to remember that *everyone* has something.

---

* In this way, perceptions and biases also swing along a continuum of severity, where they can lead to extremely critical, serious repercussions. Another case in point: black women are three to four times more likely than white women to die from pregnancy-related causes because they are perceived as having a higher pain tolerance and hence are often prescribed less pain medication than white patients who present the same complaints, and they are less likely to be recommended advanced procedures.

And it's not one particular type of person who is doing the biasing either. I've found, for example, that men and women are equally likely to be biased in favor of male entrepreneurs.

What we call bias or disadvantage is really the result of perceptions that have gone awry—when we link our perceptions about people to their attributes to describe what is "good" and "bad" in society. When, for example, blackness is linked to masculinity—but also criminality. When older age is connected to trustworthiness, but also less motivation and ability to learn. When women are perceived to be compassionate, but also incompetent.

It doesn't take much for people to form perceptions. And it takes even less for us to make attributions based on these perceptions. Psychologists Nalini Ambady and Robert Rosenthal found that even "thin-slice" encounters that last less than fifteen seconds result in strong perceptions about character—how kind, honest, and trustworthy we believe other people are.

Perceptions and attributions are made quickly. But more important, they tend to endure, even when people learn of evidence to the contrary. Once these attributions are made, they influence how others interact with you, how they assess the value you bring, and what rewards they think you deserve.

Take a look at the following chart entitled The Growing importance of Social Skills at Work, and created from research conducted by Harvard economist David J Deming. This graph adds a perspective on how we can't escape the perceptions that other people have about us, and the attributions that result. Success at work depends on social skills more today than it did in the past. There's a premium on those who are skilled in coordination, negotiation, persuasion, and social perceptiveness. These types of skills have the most potential to expose us to bias. But they also give us the most opportunities to turn inherent disadvantages into an edge. They give us the chance to guide the process of how people perceive the value we bring.

THE GROWING IMPORTANCE OF SOCIAL SKILLS AT WORK

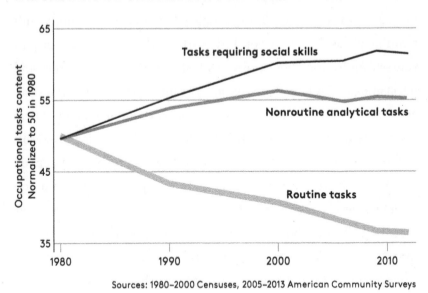

Sources: 1980–2000 Censuses, 2005–2013 American Community Surveys

"social skills": (i) coordination, (ii) negotiation, (iii) persuasion, and (iv) social perceptiveness

Don't Hate the Player, Hate the Game

Why must we take on this burden ourselves? Shouldn't the structures we have in place, and the organizations at large, be responsible for creating more equitable environments where inequality doesn't exist?

Absolutely. We should all be doing our part to change the system to get to a place where meritocracy does exist, particularly if we're in positions of power. But it's just as important to recognize that inequality isn't going to disappear anytime soon.

First, there are (and will always be) those who actively do *not* want to change the system. Unfortunately, these people tend to also be the most powerful in any given group. Research has shown that individuals—especially those who have benefited from a particular system—are prone to support and rationalize the status quo, even if there are clear problems. These people justify systemic inequity with familiar phrases like "If you just work hard enough you can pull yourself up by your bootstraps. It's just a matter of motivation and talent and grit." A branch of psychology called *system justification theory* describes how people tend to see social, economic, and political systems as good, fair, and legitimate if they have succeeded as a result of those systems. According to Erin Godfrey, a professor of applied psychology at New York University, "The people who are at the top want to believe in meritocracy because it means that they deserve their successes." Those who are in an advantaged position in society are more likely to believe the system is fair and see no reason to change it.

Second, we overestimate the extent to which people actually notice what needs to change and know how to do so, even among those who logically support change. Research shows that most successful people have a blind spot, a sort of *advantage blindness*, which can be an unintended result of system justification, but doesn't have to be. Special treatment just seems normal because it has always been their norm, and they can't imagine what the alternative would look like.

Third, even if people do fix some elements, others will remain. For example, scholars have found that increased contact between individuals can change the extent to which racial bias exists. Harvard sociologist Letian Zhang discovered that NBA players receive more playing time under coaches of the same race, even when there is no difference in their performance. As a coach spent more time with a specific player of another race, that player's playing time did increase, but the coach regressed to the original levels of bias as soon as the player was replaced by another player of the same race.

Or consider initiatives that seek to explicitly combat bias and harassment. While these initiatives may be well intentioned, researchers such as Freada Kapor Klein and Allison Scott from the Level Playing Field Institute found that the results are mixed. There is growing evidence that companies who declare that they will "just start with gender initiatives" actually set back efforts to achieve diversity along other dimensions besides gender. Creating gender parity (which often differentially benefits white and Asian women) may actually be creating increased gender-based bias, harassment, and general incivility for black and Hispanic women.

As *The New Yorker* staff writer Katy Waldman observes, "Prejudice doesn't disappear when people decide that they will no longer tolerate it. It just looks for ways to avoid detection." Let's say, for example, you switch away from standardized tests for admission because rich kids can afford prep classes. You need to realize that rich kids can also afford more sports, clubs, tutoring, and volunteer experiences.

You have to assume that the system is not going to change. But even if it does, why should you wait around for it? You can't be paralyzed by this inequity. You can't be afraid to confront the system as it is.

When you are *in the system*, you need to take charge of your own outcomes. Yes, do what you can to change systems—advocate for better hiring practices, speak up for injustice, and educate others about the reality of bias. But we can't just wait for people to make fair decisions on our behalf, make the right decisions about our future, or do things the ideal way. Creating an edge enables you to succeed within an imperfect system.

Make Your Own Privilege

Guide the perceptions that others have of you. Make your own privilege. That is ultimately how you get more out of your hard work. Just like people giving investment advice say, "Let your money make money for you," we should let our hard work *work for us*. Psychologists Shai Davidai and Thomas Gilovich describe it as *headwinds* and *tailwinds*. You need to put in the hard work. That's a must. When you create an edge, you create tailwinds that help you capitalize on your hard work more effectively. Headwinds are the biases and disadvantages that have the opposite effect, things that make it difficult for us or others to get ahead. You might still get to your destination, but it might take you much longer, it might be more painful, and you might be exhausted and frustrated by the end. Give yourself tailwinds. Allow your hard work to work for you. Turn your headwinds into tailwinds. Empower yourself by taking action—don't just sit back and let others determine that your hard work isn't enough.

It may seem inauthentic, even dishonest to do so, especially when you've been conditioned to believe that hard work is the only thing that matters. But in fact, it's the alternative that you should be wary of: allowing *other people* to decide your fate. Why should you allow others to make lazy assumptions about you based on their uninformed perceptions? Why don't you get to be the one who tells them about who you are? If you leave it up to them to "get it right," you leave a lot up to chance and are expecting a lot out of them. You leave your success up to their perceptions and attributions. Your work matters. But it is your job to help the world see how it matters.

You are dealt the hand that you are dealt, but you get to be the one to play it. There is nothing inauthentic in being dealt a hand and then deciding that you're not going to let others tell you it's a weak hand. Replace these beliefs with new ones that every successful person—regardless of their starting position or the disadvantages they face—begins with: the future can be better than the present and I have the power to make it so.

. . .

Shortly after being unceremoniously booted off the 2014 Olympic team, Nagasu wrote a message to herself describing her feelings and reflections. She later shared this with her followers in a February 2018 Twitter post:

My Fears

The articles that twist my own words into weapons and explode into me. The list of criteria I don't understand. The judgment the fans are entitled to. The people I used to look up to criticizing me. What I wear. What I eat. My body. The competing. For what?

I ask myself everyday [sic].

"Nagasu's efforts to recapture some of her old magic can be agonizing to see and hear."

Those words really push an arrow through my heart.

Everyone tells me not to listen, but, how can I not, when they jump around in my own head. To read them through someone else's words only verif[ies] my greatest fears.

My time is up.

There is no room for improvement . . .

We know about her triple axel in the 2018 Winter Olympics. What draws us to her is that she worked hard and overcame adversity. But these words are how she felt during the adversity. She was left off the 2014 US Olympic team in a controversial snub that still stings today.

Yes, she put in the hard work.

But hard work alone wasn't enough, or else she would have gotten into the Olympics in 2014. So what else was it? Being a fighter, yes. Perseverance, most certainly. But what she realized over the next four years is that making the Olympics was not solely about her hard work and skill. It was also about the *perceptions* and the *attributions* that the Olympic committee created around hard work and skill. A perception about maturity, perhaps. A perception about a unique skating program that would bring attention and interest to Team USA as one that was elite rather than passé, and what that may have meant when it was embodied by an Asian-American versus a blond American female skater.

Nagasu decided that she would guide all future perceptions about her herself. Her story wasn't about what had happened to her at the 2014 nationals, but about an athlete pushing the boundaries of her sport. Nagasu's story was about her raw athleticism, about the triple axel that she would perfect and bring into her repertoire so that she could pave her own path and give prominence to Team USA. She could create her own attributions and influence the media attention in a way that she could control, in a way that would place pressure on the USFSA to not leave her off the team again. Nagasu's monologue about her fears clearly exhibits her creative and thoughtful nature. We attribute these words to an artistic, considerate, and mature Nagasu, rather than a youthful, naive Nagasu. We attribute her hard work and effort in land-ing a triple axel to a solemn, persevering, potential Olympic medal-winning Nagasu. The jump became a key part of her plan to make it to the Olympics this time around. Once she became the captain of her own perceptions and attributions, and the perceptions and attribu-tions that she would force, using the media in her favor—that was when she created her own edge.

Though some might argue that it was just about personal brand-ing, the edge that she created for herself extended far beyond mere marketing. What did Nagasu do specifically? She knew the value she brought. She knew the value of a triple axel and how it would enrich the team. But she also knew that before people would let her in, before they would ever believe in her value, they needed to first be delighted by her story and her personality. So she let that show. She acknowledged the controversies in her career, saying, "Everybody makes mistakes and obviously I've had ups and downs." But Nagasu also declared that she had nothing to be ashamed of, owning her winding path and saying, "I'm not afraid to show everyone who I am."

And then she continued to guide that perception of her as an honest, authentic, thoughtful athlete with tweets like "You don't have to be perfect all the time. You just have to get up and keep going." So she kept going, turning headwinds into tailwinds.

Your hard work and effort work harder for you when you understand that perceptions drive the attributions that people make, which in turn drive decisions. For most of you, it will be about positioning yourselves as an antidote to stereotypes, which will allow you to guide the perceptions of others, delight others, and ultimately will result in others seeing the unique value you can provide. As we'll discover over the course of this book, figuring out your own positioning and your own contexts is what will give you *your* unique edge.

When you have an edge, effort and hard work fuel the engine more efficiently. Edge is about knowing how, when, and where to put in the effort and hard work.

The past decade of my career has been spent studying the myth of meritocracy—but even more important, studying what can be done when you acknowledge and own the fact that risk and failure work differently for different people in a world that will never be entirely fair.

I've studied what happens when you know that perception is a double-edged sword, and how you can cultivate an advantage for yourself through this awareness. And I've found that there are ways for you to actually have an unfair advantage—an edge—over others who seemingly already have an advantage, as well as those who don't yet know how to create their own edge.

Embrace it. Own it. Make it yours and turn it into an advantage. Craft it. Hone it. Make them take notice. Be that counterintuitive presence.

And as my father used to say to me as a little girl whenever I would whine about how I was so much worse than all the other kids at sports, "If you're going to play, lace up. Lace up and get ready to play." So let's get ready to play.

PRINCIPLE 1

Hard work should speak for itself.
(But it doesn't.)

PART 1

Enrich

CHAPTER 2

Your Basic Goods

Simplicity is the end result of long, hard work, not the starting point.

—Frederick Maitland

GAIN AN EDGE FOR YOURSELF, YOUR TEAM, YOUR ORGANIZATION— it's really quite simple. There are two components:

1. You bring value. You enrich what would otherwise be.

2. Others think so too.

That's it. Simple, right? But as historian Frederick Maitland suggests, the simplicity of hard work can be understood only after experiencing all the nuances.

Perhaps the most important nuance? Whether there is an *and* that connects the two components:

You bring value. You enrich.

AND

Others believe you bring value and enrich.

This is where things get sticky. Some people seem to have an edge by hitting just the second piece—that people *perceive* that they bring value—even if they don't in reality. They're just good at convincing others that they do. It's infuriating.

They got that promotion because they are always kissing up to the boss—asking about his weekend, playing squash with him—and I'm the one doing all the work that they take the credit for.

Or: How is it that our organization is getting slaughtered in sales compared to theirs when we were the first company to offer this? They were just the ruthless company who stole the ideas from us, people who were truly original, and then claimed it as their own.

Or imagine you were Henri Poincaré, who was nominated for the Nobel Prize in Physics *fifty-one* times* over the course of eight years (1904 to 1912), including thirty-four nominations in 1910 (that year there were fifty-eight nominations in total, meaning Poincaré received 59 percent of them), for his groundbreaking work in theoretical physics and celestial mechanics. But that year, the Nobel Prize went to Johannes Diderik van der Waals, who got only *one* nomination. Why didn't Poincaré receive the award? Robert Marc Friedman, a professor of history of science at the University of Oslo in Norway, explains:

Poincaré failed to secure the support of the most influential committee member, Chairman Svante Arrhenius. Largely to

---

* In a single year, different nominators can nominate the same person. A single nominator can also nominate multiple people.

oppose a rival in the academy who had initiated the campaign for Poincaré, Arrhenius pushed the candidacy of countryman Knut Ångström.

When Ångström passed away before the announcement of the prize (the Nobel Prize is not awarded posthumously), Poincaré still didn't have Arrhenius's support. Friedman continues, "Arrhenius just dug up documentation in support of Johannes van der Waals, who had long been dismissed as a candidate and whose critical research had taken place in the 1870s (despite Alfred Nobel's bequest requiring that the awards be based on achievements 'during the preceding year')." Poincaré continued to receive nominations before his death in 1912, and continued to be lauded for his scientific achievements on mass-energy relation, relativity, and gravitational waves. But he never won the Nobel.

It feels deeply unfair. For many of us, our natural instinct is to think about edge in terms of fulfilling the first component—bringing value and enriching the status quo, like Poincaré did. And that if we do a good job and show how we provide unique value, then that will be enough—people will, on their own, gather this. But they don't.

So in response, we start to feel like we need to fight fire with fire. "They kiss up to the boss? Well I can kiss up to the boss too." But in doing so, we are often setting ourselves up for more heartache and preventing ourselves from actually gaining an edge.

Once we start to focus on the extent to which people *perceive* us to provide value, we begin to minimize (and sometimes even forget about) actually providing value. We stop, to some degree, trying to enrich ourselves. We impede our own ability to bring value to the outside; we stop acquiring the tools that we might have at our disposal to even know how to enrich.

We also overlook the fact that not everybody can get away with appearing as if they provide value without actually providing it. Sure, you might know people who can get away with this strategy. There are many who can. But me? I cannot. So I don't try to do it like those other people.

To have an edge, you need to either be good at convincing others that you enrich and bring value (while not actually bringing any distinctive value), or actually bring value *and* convince them of it.

Either way, you're going to need the buy-in of others. It's much easier, it lasts longer, and it has more impact (in addition to being easier on the soul) if you achieve buy-in in such a way that you do, in fact, bring value. So we'll start there, but we will certainly, most definitely, also discuss the buy-in piece.

Delivering Value Through Your Basic Goods

What does it actually mean to enrich and deliver value?

> *en·rich* /in'riCH/
> to improve or enhance the quality or value of

What many of us subconsciously think about when we seek to *improve* or *enhance* is that we have to go *all in*. We equate value and enriching with "giving it your all."

So many of us become obsessed with going all in. We strive for it. We think that when we're good at something, we need to be so great at it that the skies part and angels sing. We're afraid to be mediocre at anything.

But seriously, isn't it enough to have just one, maybe two super-powers, and then just be okay with being *okay* at everything else?* I mean, Batman has supergenius intellect and physical prowess, but he is limited in many other ways relative to other superheroes. And Spider-Man can wall-crawl and has some admirable speed and reflexes, but he doesn't hold a candle to Superman's superhuman strength. Even superheroes are only known for one or two things.

And it's not just superheroes either. Two years ago, my husband and I took our kids on a road trip through Texas, starting off in Hous-ton (where my husband was raised and his parents still reside), then continuing through Austin, San Antonio, and other, more rural parts of the state. Before we left, my mother-in-law shouted to us, "Don't forget to stop at Buc-ee's!" I looked confused, so my husband whis-pered to me, "Buc-ee's is a gas station," which did nothing to clear things up.

But lo and behold, a couple hundred miles into the trip, we saw a Buc-ee's and my husband decided to stop for gas. And I was *blown away*. The place was a sight to be seen, a sovereign kingdom to be bowed down to. The restrooms were immaculate. Tons of fountain drinks and mountains of ice to refill our coolers. The store was packed with Texas-themed gifts that were so ingenious that I wanted to post them all on Instagram, clothing stamped with clever puns that I wanted to steal for myself, and its own brand of delicious snacks like beef jerky and caramel popcorn. I could have browsed for hours. And of course, there were rows and rows of gas pumps so that we wouldn't have to wait.

---

* This always reminds me of a bumper sticker that a friend of mine has on her car: WORLD'S OKAYEST MOM.

Captivated, I spent the next part of our car ride researching and reading about this glorious gas station. I discovered that the first store was opened in 1982 in Lake Jackson, Texas. The cofounders, Arch "Beaver" Aplin III and Don Wasek, focused on just two things: cheap ice and clean restrooms—what they called their basic goods. See, what they determined is that people go to gas stations for gas and to use the restroom (and according to Texans, to get ice for their Dr Pepper).

So Aplin and Wasek made sure that Buc-ee's had gas—that was a must. And then they focused on providing clean restrooms and inexpensive ice. And that, my friends, is how they made Buc-ee's a road trip destination. They certainly enriched my gas stop experience.

Buc-ee's in Texas City has thirty-three urinals for the guys alone. That means there is rarely a wait. The travel center has won awards for having the best public restrooms; customers marvel at how clean the facilities are, even at four a.m. The New Braunfels Buc-ee's has 120 gas pumps and a store footprint of sixty-seven thousand square feet. The location in Katy, Texas, holds the record for the longest car wash conveyor belt. Buc-ee's has more than thirty locations across Texas and is expanding to Florida and Alabama, with additional locations in development.

Though Buc-ee's began as a gas station, these days, only 60 percent of the company's revenue actually comes from gas sales, with an impressive 40 percent coming from convenience store items, including high-margin brand items. Buc-ee's has changed the way consumers think of the phrase "rest stop" because of the value it brings. In addition to gas, providing pristine bathrooms and cheap ice became the travel center's superpowers. And that allowed it to become "America's Best Bathroom," with customers bragging, "Buc-ee's is like an adult amusement park!" and "What's *not* great about Buc-ee's? Nothing!"

• • •

I've called these traits superpowers, but that makes them sound much more elusive and rare than they actually are. Enriching is really about the few things that make you singular. After all, there's nothing that complicated about big restrooms, lots of gas pumps, and plentiful ice. So I tend to think about it more as, what are my "basic goods"?

Before my Taiwanese mother begins cooking anything in the kitchen, the basic goods—the food staples that she must have—are ginger, scallions, sesame oil, and soy sauce. My Italian husband? Garlic, onions, olive oil, and cheese. (And a glass of red wine and some prosciutto di Parma for inspiration.)

Know your basic goods or the basic goods of the organizations you are leading, because they are what you will come back to, time and time again. They're the key elements that will ensure your survival, your subsistence, and your ability to truly enrich.

Ask yourself this: When people are interacting with you or your organization, what is the most basic thing they expect you to deliver in order for them to allow you to continue up the ladder of influence?

For Beaver Aplin III and Don Wasek, the basic goods were gas, ice, and clean bathrooms. With that strong foundation Buc-ee's has been able to diversify to sell food, gifts, and clothing. But it's still the basics that get people coming back.

To identify our basic goods, we must own not only our strengths but also our weaknesses. When you acknowledge and accept your weaknesses, you start to see the contours of the playing field. Knowing your weaknesses and your basic goods helps you figure out where you can create an edge.

As an entrepreneurship professor, I've often had students come to me with ideas for start-ups. Some of their ideas are quite good—for example, one student had an idea for a venture that would help bridge the gap between the time a 911 call is placed and when an emergency medical responder arrives at the scene by providing a technology that would allow the EMT or ambulance driver to communicate by video with the patient. Video communication would console the patient and allow the EMT to see the extent of any injuries and learn in advance about any preexisting conditions.

Other ideas were more mundane but nevertheless clever, like an app that would help you track credit card promotions and annual fees and help you make efficient decisions about which of those airline credit card offers to toss and which to pursue.

Regardless of the idea, many of them begin their pitch with "I've got this awesome idea" and then finish by asking, "Can you help me find a technical person who can help me with it?"

The student with the 911 idea? A background in finance—no knowledge of medicine or technology. The student with the app idea? A background in medicine—nothing in finance or technology. How can you gain an edge without grasping the basics?

This is not to say that ideas can't come from random inspiration— they certainly can. But each time I hear that an entrepreneur is looking for someone with skills that they themselves do not possess but that are the crux of what they are trying to do, I can't help but think they are not finding and cultivating their edge and their ability to enrich. They are overlooking their own basic goods.

Imagine someone came to me and said, "I have the most amazing idea for a best-selling novel. And now I just need to find a writer to write it." Or "I have the best idea for a masterpiece painting. And now I just need to find a painter to paint it." It's the same thing.

If you believe that your idea is the idea of the century, yet it relies on programming and you are not a programmer, be self-aware and admit to yourself that you will need to build that muscle.* You offer not just your strengths but also your weaknesses.

When you've discovered and pinpointed your weaknesses as well as your strengths, you've figured out where you've got an edge. You know not only where you're valuable, but where you're invaluable. Warren Buffett, American businessman and investor, chairman and CEO of Berkshire Hathaway, and third-wealthiest person in the world, describes it as understanding his circle of competence, which helps him avoid problems, identify opportunities for improvement, learn from others—and enrich.

Each of us, through our own unique experiences, has built up useful knowledge in certain distinct and finite areas. Some areas are more generic, but others are more specialized. Thomas Watson, founder of IBM, once said, "I'm no genius. I'm smart in spots—but I stay around those spots." That's the circle of competence. The image below, adapted from the Farnam Street Blog, captures and represents this idea of a circle of competence—that there is a limit to what you truly know, and that there is a dangerously exaggerated boundary of what you think you know. That gap between is where the trouble lies, but also where true value-add can be found.

Buffett once described the circle of competence of one of his managers, a Russian immigrant he called Mrs. B. "She doesn't understand

---

* One of the most unpopular pieces of advice I give to students is this: If your idea hinges in any way on technology, you have to be an expert in technology. That is not to say you need to go back to college and major in computer science. But take a four-hour crash course in programming, perhaps. If the "masterpiece" part of your idea relies on something that you are not the master of, and you can't stomach even a four-hour crash course, it is probably not the right thing for you. You ultimately won't have an edge.

stock . . . She understands furniture." He remarked that "she wouldn't buy a hundred shares of General Motors if it was at fifty cents a share"— but not knowing the stock market didn't matter. Mrs. B built the largest furniture store in all of Nebraska by focusing on her basic goods. She understood that it's not the size of the circle of competence that's important; it's knowing its boundaries. Know your weaknesses so that your weaknesses never become a liability. That's when your strengths have the opportunity to shine the brightest.

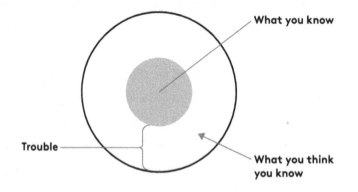

When we figure out our basic goods, it answers the essential question: Where should we devote our limited time in life to achieve the most success? Charlie Munger, Warren Buffett's right-hand man, fittingly offers the following: "Figure out what your own aptitudes are. If you play games where other people have the aptitudes and you don't, you're going to lose."

Less Is More

The trifecta of bigger, better, and more extreme—we are a society obsessed with bigger. In business, we seem to always be talking in some way about striving to be like those who seem larger than life—Larry and Sergey of Google fame, Apple's Steve Jobs and Steve Wozniak, Sir Richard Branson and his Virgin empire, Jeff Bezos and his own empire that is Amazon, the Tata family, Jack Ma and the mythical Alibaba . . . I could go on and on.

But what we don't hear is how often they themselves—these mythical unicorns such as Bezos and Ma—talk about *their* basic goods and the core products and services they arranged for their companies. These icons know that it's the basics that enabled them to get big, yet we get in trouble because we keep trying to emulate them and go for *more*. Nearly all of them, despite their spectacular growth and size, succeed because they still abide by the notion of excelling at a few things, instead of achieving mediocrity by trying to do everything.

What if we take just one of them, like Richard Branson? What we would see at first glance is what he has done with his huge Virgin conglomerate. He has his hands in air travel with Virgin Atlantic and space travel with Virgin Galactic, not to mention his presence in music and entertainment, health and wellness, and financial services, just to name a few.

But if we take the story of how Branson founded Virgin Atlantic, we soon find that he absolutely started with the basics—and further, that as he grew the company, he continued to maintain its basics. How did he start the company? With a single Boeing 747 flying between London's Gatwick Airport and Newark International Airport, in New Jersey. Now, mind you, he could have started with a whole fleet of planes and multiple routes, but he didn't. Why? Because he was testing out what he saw as Virgin Atlantic's circle of competence: the flying experience.

Billionaire entrepreneur Richard Branson* started the airline on somewhat of a whim. He was scheduled to take a flight (coincidentally enough, he was trying to get to the British Virgin Islands), but it was canceled. Needing to get to his destination, he did what most of us would do† and hired a private plane to get him there. While on the phone booking the private plane, he was asked by the booking agent, "And how many passengers will there be?" which made him realize that, indeed, there were other passengers who also needed to get to the Virgin Islands. "Hold on," he said, and (jokingly, he says) wrote "Virgin Airlines" on a board, rounding up other passengers. One version of the story holds that he charged thirty-nine dollars each, writing "$39 one way to BVI" on the board. Another version claims that he did not name a price, and in fact, there were so many other passengers interested that he started a bidding war and actually made money from the private charter.

Nevertheless, both versions maintain that Branson and the other passengers had so much fun on that flight together that something dawned on him: he was fed up with other airlines and the experience they offered. He made a phone call to Boeing, bought a 747, and tried out his hypothesis: that air travel could be an enjoyable and special experience, and that Virgin could be the one to provide it in a way that was affordable for the customers and profitable for the company.

An airline was born. It wasn't basic in its offerings—it featured mood lighting, comfortable leather seats, individual TV screens, and

---

* Incidentally, does anyone know what Richard Branson's very first company was? It was a publishing company. I discovered that his first love is poetry. He would write poems and send them to magazines trying to get them published. And he kept getting rejected. So he decided to start his own magazine, where he got to decide what got published and what didn't; he published his poems and the works of others.
† Sarcasm font.

an extensive selection of in-flight entertainment options, all before other airlines—but they distilled the "basic good" that they offered into one thing.

Still not convinced? How about what Steve Jobs did with Apple? This is a company whose signature product, the iPhone, helps them reach between $89 billion and $93 billion in revenue per *quarter*. I have never heard the iPhone described as basic. We know it for its extensive offerings of slick features: facial recognition, bionic processors, stereo sound, burst mode, and other camera features for perfect exposures.

But what Jobs recognized was the iPhone's basic good: that it is a combination device—one that people value because it can simultaneously be used as a phone and a camera and it can access the web. When Apple launched the original iPhone, it didn't have facial recognition, bionic processors, stereo sound . . . it didn't even have cut-and-paste functionality or the ability to search contacts.

You see, Apple had no idea whether the iPhone would completely bomb. They were in absolute fear that people might not actually want or even use a device that could do several things at once. What if people never ended up using the camera feature because they felt like their digital camera took clearer and better pictures? What if they preferred using their laptop for online browsing and functionality?

So they tested what they saw as their basic good: the elegance of its all-in-one combination of offerings. And with each new iteration, with each new feature, that basic good continues to guide what is to come. With their iPhone X, Apple delivered on sleekness and elegance. And with its Apple TV+, the company stayed true to a simplified, streamlined, and elegant TV-watching experience. Without a doubt, the company will continue to roll out new products that never fail to deliver on its basic goods of elegance, simplicity, and usefulness.

We can channel Virgin, Apple, even Buc-ee's. Not getting distracted by bigger, better, and more extreme can truly provide us with a means to enrich. Creating an edge starts with pinpointing your basic goods and defining your circle of competence, and operating inside that perimeter. Of course, over time, you can work to expand your circle like Buc-ee's did. But never lose sight of the basics that are the foundation of *your* edge.

PRINCIPLE 2

It's not about giving it your all.
Your basic goods help you get it all.

CHAPTER 3

Recognition of the Incongruous

To see things in the seed, that is Genius.

—Lao Tzu

WHEN EVERYONE ELSE SEEKS THE SAME DIMINISHING REWARDS BY following the same formulas in the same way, the real prizes are inevitably elsewhere. There are other veins yet to be mined, and these require a different approach. Different markets. Different values. Different networks. Different mind-sets, informed by different life experiences. As a wise friend of mine put it, "Different isn't always better, but better is always different."

Grow Where You're Planted

Brian Scudamore never got his high school diploma. On the day of his graduation, he actually *thought* that he had, but when he walked up to collect his diploma, where his certificate should have been was a notice informing him that he had missed too many of his algebra classes and that he would need to retake the class over the summer to get his diploma.

Instead of taking the class, however, he decided to apply directly to Dawson College, a two-year program in Montreal, his hometown. He wrote them a letter imploring them to let him in, explaining that he admittedly wasn't as focused in the twelfth grade as he should have been and that he hadn't applied himself, but that he was now ready. It worked.

Later, he would end up talking his way into Concordia University, a four-year institution in Montreal (leaving there after only two years), and following that, the University of British Columbia, only to drop out once more. Turns out, college wasn't for him (even though talking his way *into* college was, apparently). But by then he had already started a junk-removal company, inspired by a beat-up old truck he saw advertising a trash-hauling service while passing a McDonald's drive-through. He thought, "I can do better than that." He formed a company, originally named the Rubbish Boys, that eventually evolved into his current company, 1-800-GOT-JUNK?, which brings in more than $200 million in yearly revenue.

Though his path to success seems straightforward, and the lack of a high school diploma seems like a distant memory, it remains relevant for Scudamore. In fact, he told me that there hasn't been a single month since 1998—the year he started the Rubbish Boys—that someone hasn't brought up the phrase "high school dropout" or "college dropout."

When he first founded the Rubbish Boys, would-be investors, from banks to friends and family, refused to loan him money, asking, "What are you doing? Where is this going? How can you get this to go somewhere when you weren't even able to get college to work out for you?"

So Scudamore made sure never to allow others to take over the conversation and assign him the label of "dropout." "I decided that I had to use it to my advantage and embrace it," he said. "No one is ever going to let me forget it, so I had to embrace it as one of my assets, just like someone else would embrace their strong quantitative skills or their communication skills." He proudly brought up his own educational history, declaring, "I was someone who learned by doing, so every move I made wasn't about dropping out. It was about clearing the way to continue doing."

The label persisted. Even five years later, as his company hit half a million dollars in revenue, he faced criticism. People would say to him, "You're a high school dropout, and now you're in the trash business. Do you really want to be in the trash business your entire life?"

Scudamore continued to own it, even doubled down on it. That bias, he said, would always be a part of how people saw him, but everyone has their own skills and talents. Now he calls his dropout status his "badge of honor." "Grow where you're planted," he said. "And now I steer people in the direction of me as a dropout—not away from it. People underestimate me because of it, and I use that to my full advantage. I plant some beautiful things out of what others think is trash."

Your history and your story are part of your basic goods. Don't underestimate where you've been planted—grow there. Or grow where the soil is less jammed with other plants and you're less likely to get crowded out.

The Longest Lines Are Not Always for the Best Rides

When I was little, I remember going to Chinatown with my parents. It was in the days before Yelp; you couldn't browse online reviews and within minutes know which four-and-a-half-star restaurants with more than two hundred reviews would most suit your taste buds.

What we did in those days when we showed up in Chinatown, unsure which restaurant to frequent, was look at the lines. My parents would find the two restaurants with the most respectable-looking (read: longest) lines and then split up, each waiting in a separate line. I would go with my father to one line, my brother would go with my mother to another, and my brother and I would serve as "runners" between the restaurants, keeping each parent informed about how quickly the line was moving. When we were close to the door of the restaurant, we were finally able to give the host or hostess our name and the number of people in our party (that was how Chinatown in New York City worked, at least in the 1980s), and the decision would be made over which restaurant we would be dining at.

"The best restaurants have the longest lines," my mother still says. For decades, that was my heuristic as well. Each year, I go back to Taiwan; the restaurant scene in central Taipei is not unlike New York City Chinatown in the eighties. And the longest line? Always Din Tai Fung, a small, understated restaurant that specializes in steamed soup dumplings called xiao long bao, and other Huaiyang cuisine. Din Tai Fung now has branches in Australia, China, Hong Kong, Indonesia, Japan, Macao, Malaysia, the Philippines, Singapore, South Korea, Thailand, the United States, the UK, and the UAE, but its original location on Xinyi Road in the Da'an District of Taipei remains the most popular and most frequented. No matter what time it is, you'll always see a line outside the dumpling house—and multiple times a year, you'd have seen me waiting in that line.

Until one day, when my husband told me that he had found another small, nondescript dumpling restaurant. I was barely listening. There are dumpling restaurants all over Taipei, I told him. We've eaten in dozens of them, and they're all fine. Fine for a normal meal, but nothing special. When we want special, we go to Din Tai Fung.

Unshaken, he continued to explain, "This one *is* special. Their dumplings are actually . . . *better* than Din Tai Fung." The horror, I thought. The sacrilege of him suggesting that it was better than Din Tai Fung. I immediately set out for this mystical restaurant.

The restaurant was extremely small; if completely full (it wasn't), it might have been able to seat ten to twelve people, uncomfortably. The "menu" had just ten to twelve items . . . but they were my go-tos, the ones that I would have ordered were I at Din Tai Fung.

And the food . . . it was better. Much better. The best soup dumplings that I have ever had, to this day. They not only tasted better, but they were also the most beautiful dumplings I have ever seen.

This nondescript restaurant,* run by a husband and wife, with no line, was better than the world-renowned Din Tai Fung. Turns out, the husband was once an apprentice at Din Tai Fung. After trying to innovate on a batch of crabmeat soup dumplings one day, he claims he was fired and could not find work anywhere else. So he steamed a basket of six dumplings in his kitchen, set up a card table outside, and sold his first basket.

I learned three things. First, trust my husband when it comes to food. (This first one, admittedly, was the most difficult to learn.) Second, the same can be said of lines in an amusement park—the best rides are not always those with the longest lines. (Can I get an amen from all the other parents who have spent hours waiting in the line for Dumbo at Disney?) And third, crowds are generally wise, but the wisdom of crowds has its limits.

---

* I wouldn't even be able to describe to you how to get there, as they have no sign, no phone and no hours posted, and have never been rated on any Yelp platform or otherwise, as far as I can tell; not to mention that I had to speak to them in my native Taiwanese dialect, as their English was nonexistent and their Mandarin shaky. But if you want to try, they're about a five-minute walk from Guting subway station in Taipei.

We tend to look where things are crowded because crowds go to the shiniest thing around. This type of herd mentality can be useful in many situations, such as when you're trying to decide what kind of phone to buy, but it can also drive an entire industry down the wrong path, like what we witnessed in the spring of 2000 during the technology stock market bubble, when the entire stock market crashed, or what ensued during the mortgage crisis just a few years ago.

But getting through a crowd is sometimes really, really hard. Sometimes developing your basic goods and making the most effective use of them is best accomplished when you can go beyond the crowd and identify something distinctive on your own—that's when really special things can happen.

Angel investors adopt the exact same premise. In my research, and in my interviews with these investors, they concede that if you look at all the same investment opportunities that every other investor has looked at, and invest in all the start-ups that everyone agrees will be a success, you will achieve some level of success. But when trying to spot that diamond in the rough—that extraordinary start-up that will perhaps provide you with outsize returns—you need to go where others are not: to opportunities that others have discounted and overlooked.

Don't Underestimate the Laggards

In 1981, a revolutionary new product—the world's first laptop computer*—was developed. This laptop, named the Osborne I, had a screen that was about the size of a normal index card, weighed about

---

* Or at least that most industry pundits consider to be a laptop, because it was truly mobile.

twenty-five pounds, and required a battery pack. The lid swiveled open, revealing a keyboard. It cost $1,795. Despite its gargantuan size and weight, it was revolutionary because it offered something that no other computer could: portability. It was portable in the sense that it could be carried on a commercial aircraft.

But despite early success, the Osborne I struggled under heavy competition. Because of the market expectations and increasing demand, competitors, such as Andrew Kay, the inventor of the digital voltmeter, and Steve Jobs, Steve Wozniak, and Ronald Wayne, who together founded Apple, all rushed to offer their own portable laptop computers. The technical minds behind these companies continued to push the product forward, and the technology behind the laptop quickly developed. Laptops became smaller and more lightweight, while their memory and processing power increased exponentially. And more players jumped on the opportunity bandwagon.

By 1986, we saw the introduction of the IBM PC* convertible, which was originally designed and built under the code name Acorn by twelve engineers led by William C. Lowe. It was the first commercially viable laptop, weighing only twelve pounds, less than half of what the Osborne I weighed. It cost thirty-five hundred dollars and featured 256 kilobytes of memory, two floppy drives, an LCD screen, space for an internal modem, and the clamshell design used in today's laptops—and it made a killing. Less than four months after IBM introduced the PC, *Time* magazine named the computer "Man of the Year."

The technology continued to progress, with folks at companies like Hewlett-Packard, Compaq, and Microsoft all wanting a piece of

---

* The "PC" stood for "personal computer," making IBM responsible for popularizing the term.

the action. Engineers developed more advancements and improvements: room for a palm rest, the inclusion of a pointing device (a track-ball), and things like touch pads, optional color displays, and built-in audio. These companies sought to tap into what marketers call the "early majority" and "late majority" customer markets. And it made sense: there was the potential for more and more money to be made as laptops became more and more mainstream.

But by the early 2000s, most of the technology companies were beginning to move on, uninterested in the laggard consumers who hadn't yet bought laptops. While they would continue to serve the customers who were interested in higher-end laptops, they saw customer interest moving elsewhere—they saw the proverbial long lines moving from laptops to tablets, supposedly the next big thing.

And yes, tablets like the iPad and Samsung tablet did become big, and the crowds were indeed moving in that direction. In the meantime, however, a relatively unknown, nondescript group of individuals at an even more unknown, unfamiliar company named Asus decided that they were interested in entering the less crowded laptop market. Asus didn't even manufacture computers; it was a supplier to established companies like IBM. But these engineers recognized something that the incumbents didn't. Going into the industry with a mind-set of "more"—more advancements, more features, and more improvements—wasn't going to be effective. The existing big players were continuing to try to improve usability and performance with better battery technology, power-saving processors, improved display screens, storage technology advancements, better connectivity, and the addition of peripherals like integrated video cameras and fingerprint sensors, to name a few.

The team at Asus decided that they could go for *less*. What they realized was that the people who were "still in line" were not people who wanted bigger and better—but they were nevertheless an important market opportunity. The people left were the laggards, those who were only now getting introduced to laptops. People such as elderly parents or grandparents who didn't need all the bells and whistles, but started to want a device that could just check email, surf the web, and maybe allow them to play a few games like Solitaire,* Minesweeper, or FreeCell. So in June 2007, Asus launched its version of a laptop. It was small and lightweight and could perform those basic goods really well. Priced at around three hundred dollars, it was much cheaper than other laptops on the market (which averaged around twenty-three hundred dollars), and it was a spectacular, smashing success. Asus continues to manufacture low-cost, low-power laptops, and industry pundits have said that if one product line can be credited with nearly single-handedly creating the entire netbook category—arguably the biggest paradigm shift in mobile computing—it was the Eee PC netbook from Asus.

• • •

A secondary benefit of going where it's less crowded first is that you can practice employing your basic goods where it's less competitive before going for the more populous markets. Starting somewhere less crowded enables you to hone your core competencies before expanding your circle of competence. It also helps you avoid the human tendency to equate popularity with excellence.

---

* Interestingly enough, old-school games like Solitaire and Minesweeper were included as part of the early personal computers for a distinct purpose. Both games were reportedly designed to teach people the skills they would need to use and become more easily familiarized with newfangled PCs. The purpose of Solitaire, for instance, was to teach people how to use a mouse and how to drag and drop, as with the cards in the game. Minesweeper was also designed to help people become familiar with a mouse—specifically the concept of right-clicking and left-clicking.

The brilliant management scholar Ryan Raffaelli captures this point precisely in his painstaking depiction of how the Swiss watch industry reemerged after being battered by low-cost competitors from Asia and the rising availability of smartphones and other devices that tell time. Raffaelli argues that watches were originally prized as complex machines created through astonishing, sophisticated Swiss engineering. Rather than trying to compete with smartphones and cheap watches for the biggest piece of the market, as many watchmakers had begun to do, Swiss watchmakers doubled down on their basic goods. They reemphasized their watches' style, deep meaning, and tradition of advanced engineering to distinguish their products from those "things we wear on our wrists." Global Swiss watch sales are now stronger than they've ever been. Though watches typically retail between one thousand and five thousand dollars, sales are actually strongest at the very top of the price pyramid; watches priced five thousand dollars and up account for nearly half the sales of the entire watch market.

Knowing your basic goods helps you spot opportunities the crowds don't see, so you can distinguish yourself from crowded fields. But it also helps you spot problems with the flashy ideas the crowds are besotted with.

A Critical Eye for Incongruity

Elizabeth Holmes, founder of a company called Theranos, was the "it girl" of Silicon Valley: attractive, well-connected, Stanford School of Engineering student. The story of the rise of Theranos, the company she founded in 2003, is perhaps already familiar; it was the basis of a bestselling 2018 book called *Bad Blood*. Holmes's company solved an incredible pain point and quickly became the darling of the entrepreneurship ecosystem. She had developed technology that could use a single drop of blood obtained from a finger prick to accurately run dozens of common tests. The only alternative was to invasively draw several vials of blood from veins.

Put simply, this technology was a huge opportunity, one that gave Holmes access to hordes of prominent investors, including venture-capital firm Draper Fisher Jurvetson and the founder of Oracle, Larry Ellison, from whom she raised more than $400 million. At its peak, Theranos was valued at $9 billion. Among those included on its board were such high-flying individuals as former secretary of state Henry Kissinger, venture capitalist Pete Thomas of ATA Ventures, and former chairman of Pharmacia Corp. Robert Shapiro. Investors, the media, and even industry players such as the Cleveland Clinic and Walgreens were smitten with Holmes and her vision for the future of blood testing.

Up until this point, the story may be hackneyed and well known. But what is not as well known is the story of a group of scientists who tried to prevent Theranos from ever coming to be.

See, in the early days, before all this was unfolding, there was a cadre of medical experts who had heard an early pitch from Holmes and couldn't get past a feeling that it just didn't make sense. What these medical experts couldn't figure out was how Holmes was able to conduct such a wide range of tests with her device by relying entirely on a drop of blood from a finger; it just didn't seem to add up. And furthermore, they couldn't determine how each of these varied tests was still within the accuracy of FDA-approved medical tests.

What these scientists knew—what was squarely within their circle of competence—was basic human physiology. A droplet of blood from a finger just isn't the same as blood that comes from a vein, they thought. That blood from a fingertip needs to have traveled through fat cells, through compartments in the human body, and into the small capillaries closest to the surface of the skin. Small molecules such as glucose can travel that path and be measured accurately enough in a blood sugar test. But other, bigger molecules, like the proteins that comprise hormones and lipids that comprise cholesterol, just couldn't be uniformly identified from blood that comes from the tip of your finger in the same way that it would be from blood taken from a vein.

Years later, these scientists had long forgotten about Theranos. But once they saw the press coverage—glowing, at first, then more skeptical as questions about the technology surfaced—their memories were refreshed. A series of articles in the *Wall Street Journal* reported that Theranos was falsifying data, reporting results from traditional machines rather than its own blood-testing devices. Federal regulators banned Holmes from working in the blood-testing industry for at least two years, and Theranos faced a criminal investigation for misleading investors.

Why was Holmes able to get as far as she did? How was it that famous, widely respected people believed in Theranos when a group of scientists knew to steer clear from the beginning? For one, Holmes was a charismatic young founder with the ability to enthrall. She was also a token female entrepreneur, to whom investors could point as an example of a successful female founder. Holmes was able to maintain a secrecy around her technology in an environment that readily permits companies to operate in "stealth mode" because of intellectual property issues. But the biggest reason? The opportunity. Millions of dollars of investor money, years of development time—all of it because of this incredible opportunity, which shrouded the incongruity.

Those who have a keen eye for the perils of innovation and are able to spot *mis*-opportunity may sometimes hold an even greater edge than those who are celebrated for being innovators. An eye for incongruity helps you recognize flaws that no one else sees. The ability to identify such mis-opportunities is about pattern recognition, or being able to "connect the dots" between all the changes in technology, demographics, social forces, markets, government policies, and other factors at play in our lives. Knowing how to recognize patterns, or pattern-match, is really about knowing how to make sure the important pieces fit together.

Pattern-matching doesn't even always necessarily require a specific field of expertise or any particular specialized knowledge. Not long ago, I was approached by an inventor who had figured out a really elegant solution to the ordinary umbrella. Think about it: umbrellas are simply an annoyance. Yes, they are useful, keeping us dry when it is wet outside. But they are also a pain. Giving it three seconds of thought, I can name several annoyances that I have with umbrellas. Walking into a building after putting your umbrella down, and you're left carrying a big soppy mess that gets everything else wet. We try to use those plastic sleeves, but really, no one wants to use them (and some of us only do when people are watching anyway). Opening umbrellas, closing umbrellas. Getting into a car on a rainy day, trying to close your umbrella while opening the door and getting in and still trying to stay somewhat dry. And let's not forget those windy days, looking like an utter fool when the umbrella blows inside out.

So when this young inventor named Sam approached me with a solution that would solve all these problems, I listened. He handed me a cool-looking prototype. Picture the handle of a Star Wars lightsaber. When you pushed a button, a high-powered stream of air would shoot out and create this pocket of air above you, shaped just like the dome of an umbrella. Water would hit this air cover and slowly trickle down the sides. Super cool, right? He had even thought of a safety mechanism, so that this air couldn't be directed into someone's eye, for example. When you were done, you'd just push the button again and the stream of air would retract. No more soppy mess. Something we can all agree we would want. And indeed, Sam had conducted dozens of focus groups, each with a resounding chorus of people saying they wanted his new-age umbrella.

Sam asked if I would invest in his company. I passed, despite how sleek it was and despite all the positive acclaim from focus group participants. A number of friends of mine who also invest in early-stage start-ups, however, did invest. A few months after the initial stock of umbrellas was manufactured and put out to market, Sam quickly realized that no one was buying.

Before I tell you why no one was buying the umbrellas, let me tell you why I didn't invest. What was it that I realized from the very beginning, that I was able to connect the dots on but that my fellow angel investors were not? Well, sometimes crappy products are meant to be crappy for a purpose. We don't *need* an elegant solution for everything. I was able to think beyond the normal annoyances of an umbrella— beyond the opportunity presented to me.

Because you know what's also a pain? It's also a pain that nine times out of ten, when it starts to rain, I don't have my umbrella with me. So I like to be able to roll into a local CVS and pick up a $5.99 umbrella. And I lose my umbrellas. All the time. It's not nearly as painful for me to lose a crappy, $5.99 umbrella as it is to lose a $199 lightsaber.

Yup, that's what the umbrella was priced at, $199. That was why no one was buying.

It was not an issue in focus groups when people were asked, "How much would you pay for this? Would you be willing to pay two hundred dollars?"

In those focus groups, people were thinking about the opportunity— the sleekness of the high-powered stream of air, the innovation of the solution, the problems it would address. They were not thinking about losing a two-hundred-dollar umbrella.

Those who have an unusual perspective and are able to identify incongruity and fundamental flaws provide an edge time and time again, saving entire programs and organizations, not to mention themselves, huge amounts of money and embarrassment.

It's not often that we hear alternative perspectives that drastically differ from our own. We tend to hang out with people who are like us, who share our beliefs, values, and habits. We associate within the bounds of where we belong. So simply being the atypical voice allows you to enrich.

After his product failed in the marketplace, Sam reached out to me again, prepared to pivot on product design. I explained why I hadn't invested and why my reasons went beyond just the design of the umbrella. Based on my feedback, Sam used his talents to venture into other markets, and he now runs a successful lifestyle business that brings in more than $2 million in revenue each year selling functional and cleverly designed baby carriers, strollers, bikes, and other baby gear, all designed with a hood that offers not only UV and wind protection but also—you guessed it—rain protection.

Hand-Squeezed Juice

The health-conscious elite agree on all the same things: eat lots of fruits and vegetables, buy only organic and free-range, and stay away from "bad" carbohydrates and gluten. You know the type—you might be the type. I'm not, as much as I try.

Juicero, founded in 2013 by Doug Evans, offered a product that resonated within this health-conscious circle: a Wi-Fi-connected juicer that would allow anyone to have freshly squeezed fruit and vegetable juice in the comfort of their own homes, with the push of a button while still in bed, or anytime. With the sleek Juicero, consumers would insert a prepackaged single-serve sleeve of chopped fruits and vegetables, and out would come a delicious, nutritious, ready-to-drink beverage (think Keurig, but for juice, and controlled from any mobile device).

Evans received $120 million in funding from prominent players like Kleiner Perkins and Google Ventures. The product was priced at $699, with fruit and vegetable produce packs at around six dollars each. Who wouldn't want this in the comfort of their own home?

Evans was not a Silicon Valley veteran, but he spoke like one and began to consider himself one, grandiosely and ecstatically gushing about his product at every opportunity. "Not all juice is equal," he once said. "How do you measure life force? How do you measure chi?"

As you are probably beginning to anticipate, a $199 umbrella is uncomfortable; a $699 juicer is unnerving. But not to those at Kleiner Perkins or Google—to them, a Wi-Fi-connected juicer was a novel opportunity. Evans enamored these investors with his miniaturized industrial-strength juicer that he maintained would one day be in millions of households, helping to liquefy fruits and veggies—raw, plant-based nutrition, as he called it. This group could not get inside the mind of those who might not want one.

But more important, they were so far removed that they had not even fathomed a key weakness—until two reporters published a story suggesting that the Juicero's produce packs could be squeezed by hand, rendering the $699 juicer completely irrelevant.

These packs of fruits and vegetables could be easily squeezed to produce juice that looked and tasted just like the juice from a $699 Juicero press. The complexity and technical engineering of Juicero's press was completely unnecessary, arising from what venture capitalist Ben

Einstein called a complete "lack of cost constraints during the design process." Basically, rich-people problems. Rich people think everyone else needs the gadgets they have. They don't try to squeeze something by hand when there is a fancy machine that will do it for them.

It took someone who wasn't in the inner circle to make this connection. Someone who was able to see differently and use and embrace these differences to think beyond the norm. The optimal solution is not always obvious.

• • •

So how do we use our basic goods to enrich?

Recognize that you can start where it's less crowded, and take your time going from inexperienced to pro. Take the time to master the basics—your own, not those of everyone around you.

Acknowledge that it takes time to get good at anything. Enjoy the process of getting better and better each day, and then you can start to enjoy the result without getting hammered down where it's crowded.

And finally, take comfort in knowing that your basic goods and your perspective matter. Whether you have unique, specialized talents and skills like the doctors who didn't invest in Theranos, or a seemingly unremarkable vantage point like the Bloomberg reporters who saw through Juicero, you can create an edge.

PRINCIPLE 3

To use your basic goods in distinct ways, go where others don't.

CHAPTER 4

The Value of Constraints

When life hands me lemons, I make chocolate cake and leave bitches wondering how I did it.

—Seen on a T-shirt

Las Vegas Coolers, Hoover Dam Coolers

Each year, my closest college friends and I try to get together for a long weekend. We all live in different cities at this point—one in San Diego, one in Wisconsin, one in Colorado, one in Ireland (we think . . . because she is an Irish fiddler traveling the world, we never know where she is at any given moment). So rather than congregating in the same location, we go to different locations each time.

Two years ago, we found ourselves in Las Vegas. Now, mind you, none of us are pro gamblers. So after some pretty pathetic attempts at the slot machines and a few measly hands of blackjack, where we jokingly concluded that one of the gentlemen at our table must have been a "cooler,"* we found ourselves at the Hoover Dam, the other draw for Las Vegas tourists.

Originally named the Boulder Dam, the Hoover Dam is now regarded as one of the most impressive feats of architecture, engineering, and construction in the world. It is on the list of National Historic Landmarks, and the American Society of Civil Engineers named it one of the United States' Seven Modern Civil Engineering Wonders in 1994. It stands at 726 feet tall, is 1,244 feet long, and is made up of five million barrels of concrete. The dam itself is 660 feet thick at its base (the equivalent of more than two football fields), enough to withstand the flow of the Colorado River and harness its power to provide electricity for and direct water to the Southwest United States.

Fascinated, I learned that before the crew could even get to work constructing the dam, they first had to tackle the enormous task of diverting the Colorado River so that they could get down to the canyon floor and start pouring the foundation. This project before the actual project took a full year and required cutting four tunnels to divert the river water.

Finally, on June 6, 1933, the first bucket of concrete was poured. The concrete was mixed on-site, transported by railroad cars, and poured through an overhead bucket system that allowed them to deliver one bucket of concrete every seventy-eight seconds.

But here's the part that I found to be most captivating: regardless of how fast the concrete was poured, it had to cool and cure in order to

---

* Coolers, I was intrigued to learn, are people thought to be employed by the casino to come and change the deck a little bit, stir the pot, and mess with gamblers who are on a hot streak. There are debates about whether coolers really exist.

be structurally stable. The enormous quantity of concrete in the dam would have taken more than a hundred years using conventional methods. (Never did I think I could be so fascinated by concrete.)

But the engineers couldn't just skip the curing process. When concrete is cured, water molecules are integrated in the microscopic structure of the cement, which in turn binds the concrete, making it much stronger. This process releases a lot of heat. So not only did they have to cut the hundred-year curing process, they had to ensure that the cooling would be even. Without balanced cooling, stress cracks would form that would weaken the dam. So even if it did cool, the concrete would crack, rendering the dam useless.

What did the crews do? They came up with an idea to pour the concrete into sectioned forms. Embedded in each section was their solution for evenly cooling the concrete: a network of pipes that would circulate water cooled evaporatively by a large redwood structure at the dam construction site using half-ton blocks of ice produced daily at the site's ammonia-refrigeration plant.

It was only after the form beneath was sufficiently cool that further forms were built and filled on top of that foundation. The temperature of the circulated cooling water was measured carefully before the go-ahead was given.

Mesmerized, I saw some of the cooling pipes that are still embedded in the concrete, which can be seen protruding from the dam. Most pipes, however, were later filled with concrete for additional strength. In all, nearly six hundred miles of steel pipe are woven through the concrete blocks. The Hoover Dam is virtually unyielding against water-pressure levels of up to forty-five thousand pounds per square inch.

And it was completed two years ahead of schedule.

Constraints as Impetus

In the previous chapter, we discussed ways to think about how the discovery of your basic goods could also lead to a discovery of how those basic goods could be employed to enrich. Constraints, it turns out, also provide us with a unique opportunity to discover and employ our strengths in a way that enriches. Constraints alter the path that we take, even in the instances in which they make us feel like we have no options.

The fourth-grade version of myself clearly recalls that feeling of constriction. It was communicated to my teacher that I had scored outrageously high on the standardized tests that we had to take each year that measured aptitude in math, reading comprehension, and language arts. Based on my scores, I had more than qualified to be in the school's Gifted and Talented program. But because up until that point no one had qualified based on test scores and students were typically placed in the program only via teacher referrals, my teacher urged the principal to give me a battery of additional tests before admitting me to the program. The scores came back, and the results confirmed the earlier indicators—I had scored extremely high in math, and even higher in both reading comprehension and language arts.

My teacher agreed that I should be placed in the Gifted and Talented program for math—but not for reading/language arts. I was the only student who was admitted into just "half" the program, attending only those sessions that related to math, and told to stay with my current class for reading/language arts. I was told that because English was not my native language, they could not put me in the program for reading/language arts. I tried to explain—as well as a nine-year-old can—that English *was* one of my native languages (and that speaking another language didn't prevent me from also being able to speak English). And hence the formation of a nine-year-old's conceptualization of constraint.

The world conspired to teach me that life rhymes, and I found myself in a similar situation my freshman year of college. After turning in my first paper for UWC, the University Writing Course that all students are required to take their first year, I received an F on the assignment. Shocked, I approached the instructor to ask him where I had gone wrong. His response was astoundingly familiar: "Don't worry, since English is not your native language, it will take you some time to get the hang of writing. It will come."

I suspect that the constraint was placed upon me based on my ethnic last name. Indeed, a few days later, I bumped into another Asian student in the class, and after a few tentative glances, we approached each other and asked how the other had done on their UWC paper. The results were consistent.*

So we came up with a plan to "own" the constraint. We decided to reference our "nonnative English" as often as possible. I wrote my next essay on the challenges of growing up as a nonnative English speaker and how I strove to overcome these challenges and saw UWC as my salvation and as the gift that would allow me to become successful. The professor detected none of my sarcasm and gave me a B-.

When we *own* constraints, magical things can happen. Indeed, when we leverage difficulties and use them as tools to propel us toward success, we start to carve out our edge. We enrich in ways that put the

---

* And years later, in an astounding study, Sonia Kang, Katherine DeCelles, András Tilcsik, and Sora Jun provided us with the proof we needed. They found that as many as 40 percent of minority job seekers "whiten" their résumés by adopting anglicized names and downplaying their race to bypass biased evaluations in an attempt to get their foot in the door.

focus on us, rather than on others—as long as we don't let others dictate our constraints, that is.

When $5 < $0

There's an exercise that I used to do with my students. I would give each team of students an envelope with five dollars inside. I'd tell them that this money was their "seed funding"—money they could use as start-up capital to create any type of profit-generating venture that they wanted. At the end of the week, they were to present their venture to the rest of the class and reveal how much they had earned in profit.

The goal of the session was for students to hone their entrepreneurial instincts by trying to identify opportunities, given the five-dollar constraint and the limited resources they were provided with. And, in fact, they were very entrepreneurial. Some of the ideas I have seen over the years: car washes that used the five dollars to invest in sponges, soap, car wax; community flea markets and tag sales that spent five dollars on advertising in return for banking "table fees" from each vendor; and bake sales built from all the ingredients that five dollars can buy. These teams all do fairly well leveraging their five dollars in exchange for decent profits* and have regularly come back with four or five hundred dollars.

---

* The one exception is a particularly fascinating team of students a few years back, who came back with no profits at all. How did they explain this in their presentation to the class? So immobilized by the five-dollar constraint, they couldn't agree on an idea that they felt would produce a profit. So they decided to focus on "quality of life" rather than "quantity of profit," and used the five dollars for a date night with their significant others. But even after deciding upon that course of action, they struggled with constraint: the trade-off whereby for five dollars, they said, "You can either get your girl approximately two flowers from a florist or you can get her an entire Costco

But the teams that made the most in profit? Those who *didn't use the five dollars at all.* It's a lesson they are all amazed to learn: that those who come back with the highest profits—one year, a team came in at over four thousand dollars—are typically the ones who never even use the five dollars. The teams that seem to generate the greatest profit are those who look at the resources at their disposal through a completely different lens.

We have a tendency to focus on constraints, even when we are thinking in terms of opportunities. We scan the environment for ways that we can provide value and we zero in on the obvious opportunities—all the ways we can use five dollars. This ends up excluding a large set of opportunities—those that we could do based on four dollars, three dollars, or even nothing. And more important, it excludes ones that we need thousands of dollars to do. You see, the five dollars actually becomes a constraint. It limits the ideas that are possible. When the focal point is the five dollars, there are only so many opportunities available to us—so we end up doing things like car washes, lemonade stands, and bake sales. That is how the majority think.

Arlan Hamilton, a venture capitalist who went from living out of her car to raising $10 million for her most recent fund, once said, "You put me at zero, [and] there is no limit to what I can achieve."

So what kinds of companies did these teams who put themselves at zero and therefore saw themselves as "constraint agnostic" start? One team, after deciding that the most valuable asset they had was, in fact, not the five dollars in their hands but their presentation slot in class, decided to sell that time to a company that was interested in recruiting students for seasonal work. The team helped the company

---

rotisserie chicken." (Yes, the roast chicken was five dollars at Costco, and yes, that one chicken was the meal for *all* of them.)

create a short commercial that was presented to the other students in the class during their presentation time.

Another team also began by thinking about what assets they had beyond the five dollars. What they decided to do was first make a list of all the talents each team member brought to the table. As they started sharing all their talents, they were intrigued by how diverse and distinctive their talents were when considered as a collective whole. So they filmed, with their iPhones, a series of commercials that formed a coherent program of offerings featuring the talents of each team member. They sent the videos to everyone they knew and told them to pass it on to everyone *they* knew, advertising a workshop where they would teach their talents. They charged each participant twenty dollars to attend, and had more than twenty attendees.

Yet another team set up a booth in the main quad offering a free service to measure bicycle tire pressure. If the tires were low on air, they could add air for one dollar. Even though air-fill stations were free at all the nearby gas stations, students were more than willing to pay a dollar for the convenience of having it done on campus. Even so, feeling a bit guilty, the next day, the team decided to stop charging a dollar and just put out a donation bucket instead. Their earnings soared.

One of my favorites was a team who hosted a "moving dinner": each course—appetizers, main course, and dessert—was at a different location, with a different set of people. At five thirty p.m., you received a text message with a location for appetizers, and you'd just show up and meet four or five people whose identity was unknown to you. Then at six thirty p.m., you'd get another text with a location for the main course with all new people, and at eight p.m., the dessert location. At the end of the evening, a text message would arrive with the name and address of a local bar where all fifty participants would meet back up. For this evening of fun, participants paid a flat fee in advance, which covered everything by way of preset menus that my students arranged with each eating establishment. The students kept the profits. The problem they identified and aimed to solve: networking isn't always fun; meeting new people isn't always easy.

A few weeks after the course ended, I received an invitation from one of the members of this team: the moving dinner had been such a success that they decided to make it a monthly event and were in the process of coordinating the next one, and would I consider attending? (I did.)

You Don't Need $5, or Even 6–8 Years of Experience

Constraints don't have to be constraining. Those who assumed that they had nothing in start-up capital did better. They didn't see the five dollars as a crutch, and focused on the opportunity instead of the constraint. That freed them up to think about what other assets they did have, and pushed them to look beyond five-dollar problems to more valuable opportunities. If we let others dictate our constraints—that we must use the five dollars—then we can't dictate our own opportunities.

One student said it best: "Don't follow the money, follow the worth." (There's a difference.) This thinking applies to us as individuals too. We have a tendency to let others dictate our constraints, shackling us and preventing us from thinking beyond those constraints. We focus on our weaknesses, the skills that we don't have.

This is backed by scores of studies. When people apply for jobs,*

---

* Women, in particular, most often fall into this trap, though it has been found that more than 40 percent of men didn't see themselves as meeting the qualifications and therefore didn't bother applying for an otherwise perfect job.

more often than not, they determine that they are not qualified for the positions. So they never bother applying, even when they have identified those jobs as ones they would absolutely love.

You find an incredible opening, but it asks for six to eight years of experience and you only have four, or it's in a different industry than you're in now, or there are a few bullet points in the job description that you've never done before.

Instead, go beyond the constraints and look for the opportunities. Do you fit at least three of their criteria? If so, try to find a way to emphasize why the criteria that you do fit are so important. Others create constraints—we shouldn't impose additional constraints on ourselves; instead, we should hunt for the opportunities where we can enrich.

We are trained to look at defined problems. But in life, problems are undefined. A team of clever researchers from Washington University in Saint Louis, Markus Baer, Kurt Dirks, and Jackson Nickerson, has examined precisely this point: that we often actually constrain ourselves because we don't give enough attention to problem *formulation*. One way we constrain ourselves is by not formulating problems in a way that we can actually solve them and hence provide value. We constrain ourselves by not formulating the true problem.

Take, for example, a high-growth start-up that I was advising, whose sales were starting to stall. The founder was concerned that his product, a suite of services that helped large manufacturing firms manage their processes, was no longer an attractive offering. He wanted my help in identifying new product features to add. I could have gone directly to the product team to discuss additional innovations, but instead, I sat down with members of his team to talk through the entire sales process. To our surprise, we found that declining sales were due to one particular aspect of the process—the final step. We found that the sales team was having difficulty sticking to the price that they had negotiated with the customer, and was offering additional features in an effort to test out higher prices. What was assumed to be a product issue was in fact not a product issue at all.

We tend to focus on solving problems and generally are decent at it. We look for people who can create valuable solutions to strategic problems. We bring together people from heterogeneous backgrounds and disciplines, trying to form top teams with cross-functional and interdisciplinary strengths. But much of this is in vain because before we can effectively create valuable solutions to strategic problems, we need to know what problem we should be addressing in the first place.

Let's say you were tasked to design a car for automobile racing, the kind that's used in Formula One, for example, or NASCAR (the actual vehicles for these races differ). This is the exact problem that many motorsport engineers are presented with—and indeed, what do most engineers aim for? Building the fastest car possible. The best way to beat another car is to have the fastest one, right?

By reframing the problem and not jumping to solutions, Audi's chief engineer took a different approach. He asked, "How might we think about winning Le Mans* if our car is not the fastest?" By considering this question instead, his design team came up with a new solution: a fuel-efficient car, which reduced the number of pit stops and allowed them to offset not being the fastest car, helping Audi win the prestigious race four years in a row.

The conventional notion that we tend to "jump to conclusions," more precisely stated, is that we tend to "jump to solutions." That's what

---

* The twenty-four-hour Le Mans race, the world's oldest active sports car race, has been held annually since 1923 near the town of Le Mans, France, and is considered one of the most prestigious automobile races in the world. Le Mans represents one leg of the Triple Crown of Motorsport, in addition to the Indianapolis 500 and the Monaco Grand Prix.

we learn in school. As students, we are given predetermined work to complete, predetermined cases to consider. In organizations and in the world outside schools, much of the work itself entails determining what the work and the problems actually are.

What the scholars from Washington University suggest is that to avoid jumping to solutions, formulating problems has to be more deliberate, and specifically, deliberated through two distinct phases: first, framing and identifying the symptoms, and only after that, formulating problems.

Translating from academic-speak, in the words of my wise friend Stan van Bree: "Don't make your f*#&ing problem my f*#&ing problem."

Lean into constraints. Enrich by accepting and embracing constraints, rather than trying to duck or dodge them. Don't let the constraints that others create prevent you from identifying the problem for *you*, and hence the solution for you. Allow constraints to help you enrich. Use them in your favor. When you treat constraints differently than others, you will have the edge.

Constraints can be a benefit and source to be leveraged to enrich— so much so that *not* having them can also create problems, resulting in an even lesser chance of enriching and providing value.

Corporate Incubators

In 1959, in a Batavia, New York, warehouse, Joseph L. Mancuso opened the Batavia Industrial Center, considered to be the very first business incubator. His goal was to provide a space that would serve as a shared location for companies to "incubate" their ideas and innovations, providing economies of scale on resources that these companies usually lack, such as access to legal, accounting, computer services, funding, and other services.

Incubation expanded in the United States in the 1980s and spread to the UK and Europe through various related forms, such as innovation centers, *pépinières d'entreprises*, and technology and science parks. Around that time, corporate incubators, a particular breed of business incubators, began to crop up. These corporate incubators are run within the confines of one specific corporation. Many large corporations now have one—Intel has one (Intel Capital), Google (Google Ventures), Facebook (Facebook Start-up Garage), Salesforce (Salesforce Ventures), Lockheed Martin, DuPont, Coca-Cola, Lowe's, Oracle, even Walmart (called Store No. 8, in homage to an early location where Walmart experimented with store layouts).

The executives behind corporate incubators buy into the idea that such a system makes it easier to ideate and test concepts. Through their incubators, they can offer a company the potential to channel fresh ideas and innovation from outside into the traditional organization. These companies can use their resources to attract innovators and creative people, and because the incubator is outside the traditional ivory walls, they can more easily develop a culture that fosters ideas and experimentation.

Incubation teams are able to come up with innovative ideas that fit the current business models and capabilities of their sponsoring corporation, and these types of innovations can easily be transferred from the incubator back to the corporation. The corporation can then use its existing structures and large resources to rapidly exploit the new business opportunities at scale.

All this sounds great, right? Good ideas and good intentions, but here is the deal: they don't work.

Why not? Truly great companies are born in garages, where individuals have a sense of urgency, dread running out of cash, are trying to hustle to get the product out before competitors, and live with an uncertainty about whether their product will resonate with customers, or if they have even targeted the right customers. In a word, it comes down to *constraint*. Corporate incubators are less successful because they don't have constraints, and not having constraints creates problems with innovation.

Companies that are a part of corporate incubators? What researchers have found is that these incubators know that they are backed by corporate funding, know who their customer is and (think they know) exactly what they want, and can go home at five p.m. if they want. They don't face any of the dread and trepidation that start-up founders face.

The corporations themselves massively overestimate their knowledge of what types of innovation they are looking for. Google Ventures, for example, might communicate to their incubator start-ups that they should be seeking solutions that help organize the world's information and make this information universally accessible and useful. Google dominates 75 percent of the US online search market, and every month millions of unique users perform billions of searches, so start-ups in their incubator work on ideas in this vein.

Start-ups quickly realize that most of the great ideas or valuable business opportunities they uncover will slowly die in the sponsoring corporation. The ideas that they uncover don't fit into the existing value streams, customer experiences, or business capabilities; perhaps they can't be effectively imitated within the larger company structure— or worse yet, they cannibalize existing products within the sponsoring corporation. The start-ups in Google Ventures, for example, then discover that the company has spent $1.65 billion acquiring YouTube, $996 million acquiring Waze, and $3.2 billion acquiring Nest Labs.

They begin to think: You told us to focus on online search, and yet you spent billions acquiring companies that are in the business of video sharing, traffic patterns, and temperature and humidity control?

At this point, corporate incubators have achieved the opposite of their intent. They have weakened the innovative strength of a corporation. The absence of the very constraints that incubators set out to help start-ups avoid prevents their ability to enrich and create value.

• • •

Constraints limit and control what we can do. They are an inevitable part of life, and rather than ignore them, we can discover and pay attention to them. What we often fail to recognize is the value of constraints. In many ways, we *need* them. When we notice constraints but don't let them define our possibilities, we can actually flip them to create an advantage.

PRINCIPLE 4

Embrace constraints.
Constraints provide opportunities.

CHAPTER 5

Honing Your Gut Feel and What You Bring to the Table

If I had eight hours to chop down a tree, I'd spend six hours sharpening the ax.

—Abraham Lincoln

WHILE GETTING MY HAIR CUT THE OTHER DAY, I NOTICED MY hairdresser, Jennie, spending just a few seconds longer than expected, examining a bruise that I had developed on the right side of my head, right at the hairline. She innocently inquired, "Oh my, what happened?"

In the level of detail that I normally reserve for my hairdresser, I began to tell her, "I was making the bed in our guest bedroom, but one side of the bed is against the wall, so it's never easy for me to get the fitted sheet on smoothly on that side. In any case, in trying to get the fitted sheet on I hit my head on part of the headboard and cursed a little too loudly . . ."

Jennie quickly lost interest in my explanation (and then pointed out a few strands of gray that were apparently new) and began to tell me about something she had heard from a friend of hers, also a hairdresser, who lives in Chicago.

"Did you know that hairdressers in Illinois are now required to attend domestic violence and sexual assault training?" she asked. Surprised, I inquired, "Are hairdressers more often victims of domestic violence than normal?"

They are not, it turns out. But Jennie told me that victims of domestic violence are more likely to open up to their hairdressers and share details when they have been assaulted. Because hairdressers and salon workers often have a unique ability to develop close relationships with their clients, it puts them in a rare position to ask questions when they notice something amiss, and even identify and offer help to victims.

Kristie Paskvan, founder of *Chicago Says No More*, a regional group in Illinois seeking to raise awareness about domestic violence, echoes, "When someone is essentially grooming you, you build a relationship with them. . . . It's a special relationship. People open up."

This gave activists an idea: mandate that hairdressers and licensed beauty professionals attend domestic violence and sexual assault training so they can learn to spot signs of abuse. The training, which started in 2017, isn't intended to turn hairdressers into counselors or therapists— but it helps equip them so that they can recognize signs of domestic violence in their clients, serve as a supportive ear, and be prepared to share resources and refer them for support services* if needed. They aren't expected to offer counseling, and they are not legally required to report abuse even if it is disclosed to them, but their help can go a long way toward prevention.

I love how inventive and resourceful it is. At its core, this program

---

* In the United States, call 1-800-799-SAFE (7233) for the National Domestic Violence Hotline.

gives victims a way to be recognized, receive critical information about help that is available to them, and potentially prevent future episodes and save their lives. And it acknowledges that great ideas come from the ability to intuit the unexpected.

Gut Feel and the Exponential Function

These hairdressers ask questions, listen, make connections, and in so doing save lives. How? "We just use our intuition," says my hairdresser, quite simply.

"Using your intuition" sounds simple, but it's harder to pinpoint what that means. Some, especially decision scientists, say that intuition is completely irrational, and hundreds of years of science tell us that making a decision based on your gut is emotional and illogical and leads you to biased outcomes. In fact, I once received this feedback after I submitted my first paper on the role of gut feel in business to a scholarly outlet:

> I find the entire paper to be problematic. Examining "gut feel"—something that is a slang word and should be reserved as such—is a complete waste of time and it was a waste of my time to read this work. We strive for theoretical impact in our field, and this paper is what I would define as atheoretical.

(This feedback was through a blind review process, if you couldn't tell.)

Admittedly, I took that feedback to heart. I would have abandoned all my research on gut feel entirely if it hadn't been for a couple of marvelous scholars at the University of Maryland, who, as luck would have it, invited me to present my work just days later. Timidly, as you can imagine, I gave the presentation. The response was something that I have never forgotten: immediately after my talk, they told me that my work was "cutting-edge" and daring and asked me to promise to never give up this line of research.*

My research on gut feel reconceptualized the way we think about intuition. I found that rather than subconscious or "irrational"— feeling without thinking, or "below the surface of consciousness," as Malcolm Gladwell asserted in his 2005 book, *Blink*—what we describe as gut feeling is actually emotional *and* cognitive. There is feeling with thinking, and "going with our gut" need not imply uncertainty and flawed decisions.

Let me be more precise. Gut feel is what happens on the boundaries, at the extremes. When we are making a normal decision, one that is routine or conventional such as which washer and dryer to purchase or which job candidate is most qualified for a particular work task, we don't need our gut feel, and in fact, sometimes our gut feel *does* lead us down erroneous paths. But when we need to make decisions that are anomalous and idiosyncratic, gut feel is invaluable.

To illustrate: I found that angel investors who use their gut feel are more likely to identify the home runs—the firms that will return them thirty times their investment or more. Their gut feel doesn't help them on an overall, will-I-end-up-in-the-positive-or-in-the-negative kind of way, like someone who puts $200 into the stock market to try to make $220 at the end of the day. It helps them when they are willing to put in $200 and risk losing it all so that they might end up with $20,000.†

---

* Thank you, Brent, David, and Rajshree; I am indebted.

† Not to say that a different type of bias isn't a factor in these instances—and that is where things get tricky, because embedded within one's gut feel is the potential for the systematic disadvantaging of others. We must also watch for that.

In baseball terms, your gut feel won't help you achieve a higher batting average. You might end up with a .125, but you're going to have achieved that through home runs, not singles or even doubles.

Gut feel is simply the combination of your own experiences and your unique ability to make connections in nonlinear, non-incremental, and hence unexpected and delightful ways.

As the physicist Albert Bartlett once said, "The greatest flaw of man is not being able to fathom the exponential function." We tend to think linearly and are seldom able to conceive of a better way—the exponential function. Management scholars Robert Costigan and Kyle Brink describe linear thinking as rule based, superficial, logical, and easy to replicate. If linear thinking is about doing things one step at a time in a straight line, exponential thinking is about visualizing things in leaps and bounds and zigs and zags. When you think linearly, you underestimate what is actually possible. When you start thinking exponentially, in a way that cultivates your own personal experiences *plus*, it becomes one of the most powerful ways to hone and practice enriching.

Exponential thinking is behind innovative initiatives such as Illinois's hairdresser training, but also mundane (yet revolutionary) products such as the disposable diaper. The diaper doesn't need much of an introduction—essentially a type of "underwear" that absorbs and *contains* waste (known as the "insult" in diaper speak, I kid you not). Diapers are typically made either of cloth (layers of fabric such as cotton, hemp, bamboo, microfiber, or even plastic fibers such as PLA or PU, which can be washed and reused) or synthetic disposable materials.

Diapering can actually be traced back to 1590s England, but the disposable diaper only reached its modern form—and really started to enrich lives—in the 1940s. In 1946, a woman named Marion Donovan decided to use a shower curtain from her bathroom to create a plastic cover to go on the outside of a diaper. This plastic encapsulation (later named the "boater") was the origin of the disposable diaper as we know it today.

The story goes that Vic Mills—who was a chemical engineer for Procter & Gamble and worked not only on the modern disposable diaper (what would later become the Pampers brand), but also on Pringles chips, Ivory soap, Duncan Hines cake mix, and a host of other products—came to the realization that stuffing the plastic that encapsulated diapers with wood chips increased the diapers' absorbency. The diapers would not only hold the insult but also partly absorb it. These wood chips were sliced in a special way that allowed them to increase absorbency while taking up minimal space within the diaper—in fact, they were sliced in the same way that Pringles chips are still sliced to this day.

Then, in the 1980s, Carlyle Harmon, an American who was head of fabrics research for Johnson & Johnson, and Billy Gene Harper, who was working at Dow Chemical, discovered that they could stuff the plastic encapsulation with superabsorbent material from polymers—the same material that is now used to clean up oil spills.

Bricolage

Connections, linkages, Pringles, oil spills. Over the next few decades, the disposable diaper industry boomed—all predicated on the advancements and innovation made through the linkages that Vic Mills and Harper and Harmon identified. What Vic Mills, Harper and Harmon, and even Donovan did was engage in bricolage, the creation of something novel and exciting from the combination of our personal experience and our contexts. In art or music or literature, bricolage refers to construction or creation from a diverse range of available things—like a punk rock band reinterpreting classical music. In business, companies use things they have on hand, recombining them in nontraditional ways to produce valuable new products and innovation—like Airbnb did when it combined lodging services, accommodation seekers, smartphone and location technology, and payment-platform infrastructure.

My favorite way to understand bricolage, though, is probably through *MacGyver*, the TV series that I used to watch as a kid.* Mac-Gyver ("Mac"), the show's protagonist and a splendid, charming guy, is asked to solve all these problems in the world. In one episode, there might be a vial containing a deadly virus that is stolen from a science lab and MacGyver needs to recover it. In another, Mac and his team might be called upon to break up a massive counterfeiting ring. Regardless, it is some world-altering situation—he has to stop some bad guy who is trying to bomb the entire world, for example. So over the course of a one-hour episode, he has to use his intellect, knowledge, and his general collection of skills to do something. So he'll be like, "Ooh, a paper clip . . . and look, a match and a wad of chewing gum . . ." He'll assemble each of those random things in a clever way, and then in the last thirty seconds of the episode he'll push a button, the bomb will fizzle and defuse, and the world will be saved.

That's bricolage. It's taking what you have on hand and putting it together in an innovative, improvisational way to do something really special. Companies that can do it are able to go beyond their resource

---

* I am told the show has made a comeback—in a reimagining of the classic action-adventure series that I remember so fondly, MacGyver works for a clandestine government organization using the cover of a think tank.

limitations—their constraints—and challenge institutional barriers and limits to seemingly create something from nothing.

To make these kinds of linkages and reap the benefits of our personal experiences *plus*, sometimes the *plus* must come to us through formal training, like the type that Illinois hairdressers are receiving. And though successful bricolage doesn't always come from the disadvantages, the pains, and the struggles that we've experienced, we have it within us to unearth the *plus* and the patterns through obstacles and adversity. When we do so, it can present a particularly valuable means to enrich. The rest of this chapter explains how we can hone our ability to see these opportunities.

Your Frustrations Are Others' Frustrations

In 1989, Michael Eidson, an avid bicyclist, was competing in the Hotter 'N Hell 100 bike race in Wichita Falls, Texas. Annoyed with the water bottle holder on his bike and its location (which required him to awkwardly lean down to grab the bottle, open the bottle while drinking, close it up, and return it to the same inconvenient location), Eidson decided to jury-rig a solution. An EMT by trade, he went to his ambulance and found a sterile IV bag and tubing. He proceeded to fill the IV bag with water and then stuck it in a tube sock, pinning the sock to the back of his jersey. He then pulled the tube over his shoulder and secured it with a clothespin. This was the prototype of the CamelBak hydration pack. That's bricolage in action.

Within months, the pack caught on. Eidson refined it into a compact, slim container that would feel light and stable and create minimal wind resistance. He began selling his invention, which allowed people, for the first time, to carry water on their backs, giving athletes a more convenient and efficient way of drinking during physical activities. No longer did athletes need to stop or even slow down to clumsily fumble with bottles for their water; they could simply grab the drink tube connected to the water reservoir inside the backpack (I was amused to discover that this water reservoir is called a bladder).

Nowadays, there are multiple types of hydration packs, designed specifically for all different types of activities, be it long-distance hikes, bike rides, or snowboarding. Packs differ in terms of size (small for short hikes to ones that are big enough for ultralight overnights), capacity (how much space you want for your water and your gear), fit (making sure the pack fits your body type, torso length, hip size, and so on), and even extra features like bite valve on-off switches and quick-connect tubing.

What Eidson did was address a personal pain point. Pain points are problems, plain and simple. And if you have a problem, many others probably do too. Inspired by both his EMT and cycling backgrounds, Eidson created a product that quickly became popular among cyclists*—as well as other types of athletes and outdoor enthusiasts. His product was even used by soldiers and troops in battle as a

---

* Another wonderful illustration of pattern-matching and innovating on what you know also comes from the cycling world. Have you ever wondered why the PowerBar has that chewy, sticky, almost rubbery texture, and why its texture is so different from other bars on the market? The story goes that the inventors of the PowerBar found it quite annoying to have to figure out what to do with the granola bars that they would bring along on bike rides. They had to open the wrapper, and then they would take a bite, only to have to figure out what to do with the rest of the granola bar if they wanted to save it for later. So they went into their kitchen and developed the first formulation for the PowerBar. With that thick and sticky texture, they could peel it open and take a bite, then wrap it around their handlebars and bike some more. When they got hungry again, they could peel it off their handlebars and take another bite, then wrap the rest around the handlebars again. Kind of disgusting, but also superbly innovative.

"personal hydration system" during the first and second Gulf Wars as well as the War in Afghanistan. US and foreign government contracts now make up more than 40 percent of CamelBak's business.

Getting to the extraordinary, the exponential, is not as difficult as we might imagine. It is based on what we already know. Eidson knew cycling and he knew his ambulance supplies. The problem is that we often create barriers to thinking exponentially. We think about losing five pounds, and then ten pounds, and then more, rather than thinking about altering the way we think about health and wellness. We employ company strategies to achieve incremental growth—through products that are incrementally improved over prior ones, prices that are incrementally better, processes that are incrementally upgraded, or talent that is incrementally more experienced. Luckily, there are ways that we can practice and hone our ability to be extraordinary and to think exponentially, and in doing so truly enrich.

Inversion as the Antidote to Self-Doubt

Non-incremental, exponential thinking often occurs when we "flip the formula." When we invert, or upend, or turn something upside down, it allows us to identify and remove obstacles to success. As a tool for developing our ability to enrich, it means approaching a situation from the opposite end of the natural starting point.

Returning to my work on gut feel, and taking my publishing woes as an example, most of us, me included, think one way about a problem: forward. The problem I faced, much as I didn't want to admit it, was that even if my ideas surrounding the true value of gut feel were sound, I quite honestly had no idea how to write an academic paper.

Academic writing, I discovered, was a whole different type of writing from what I had learned. Riddled with self-doubt, I reached out to a prominent scholar in my field and quite vulnerably admitted, "I'm worried that I'm a fluke and that I'll get nothing but rejections." He replied, "I had eighteen rejections before I had a single acceptance." Now, I have come to learn he has never admitted this to anyone else, so I have no idea why he decided on that day to admit it to me. Nevertheless, that evening, as I thought about his admission, I inverted the problem I was facing. Rather than striving for paper *acceptances*, I decided to endeavor for *rejections*—eighteen, to be exact.

I decided that if this famous, prolific scholar had started his career with eighteen rejections, well, then why shouldn't I? Learning something like this just takes time, and most people stop because they are paralyzed by failure. And sometimes it's getting through the failure (and even coming to terms with it) that allows you to get to where you need to be. I decided I would give myself space to learn and improve. I would also aim for eighteen rejections before expecting a single acceptance.

I received fourteen rejections and four revise-and-resubmits (the closest to an acceptance that you can reach in my field, at which point you are invited to resubmit until it ultimately is rejected or accepted). I was exhausted, but I committed myself to keep going until I had a total of eighteen rejections (never mind the number of acceptances). When the next paper I submitted was *not* a rejection, I was surprised. But I was even more surprised by what I had tracked across all my submissions. Across those fourteen rejections and five acceptances, I discovered patterns. Patterns about certain papers that accounted for multiple rejections—patterns that helped me build a gut feel about which projects I should just kill early on and which projects to hunker down on and push through.* Patterns about particular coauthors who all but ensured rejection—patterns about whom I worked well with and whose skill sets complemented mine (and whose did not).†

Flipping the situation around and thinking backward allowed me to develop my strategy—the same strategy I use to this day. I work on only one paper in earnest at a time (unlike others who might have six or seven going at one time in an attempt to protect themselves from acceptance rates that can be 10 percent or lower) and try to convert each and every paper. If a paper doesn't seem like it's getting the traction I want, or the findings are not robust, I kill it off immediately. And so on.

Inverting one's thinking means recognizing that while sometimes it's good to start at the beginning, it can be more useful to start at the end. It means thinking about how you will manage and fulfill a big contract *before* getting the contract, so you can formulate the terms and the discussions.

For companies, it means thinking less in terms of problems in search of solutions and more in terms of solutions in search of problems.

3-D Printing and Solutions in Search of Problems

To demonstrate the difference between problems in search of solutions and solutions in search of problems to my students, I ask them to participate in a thought experiment. I explain what a 3-D printer

---

* For example, I learned that though the advice I had been given was to build on the work of others and not go for a topic that was "too provocative," my pattern was the opposite—provocation led to interest, which led to attainment.

† Again, these were trends and patterns that I would never have intuited otherwise. Case in point: when I collaborated with those who were recognized as prolific scholars and experts in how to publish, I actually did much worse than when I collaborated with peers who, like me, were still trying to figure it out.

is—something that can make pretty much anything*—and then give them the following parameters: with your 3-D printer, you can produce anything the size of a microwave or smaller; you can assume a one-dollar cost for the materials and manufacturing of any one item; and the final product is to be sold for a profit.

I tell them to brainstorm any idea that they can come up with for a commercial product. Try it yourself. Take a few minutes to come up with a list of your own.

After a period of time, we discuss their ideas—but not before I conspicuously place a sealed envelope at the front of the room and tell them that in the envelope I have written down what I predict they will come up with. I then write all their ideas on the board. Here are some of them:

- Car parts
- Jewelry
- Sunglasses
- Toys
- Musical instruments
- Medical and dental parts
- Replacement parts
- Architectural models and layouts
- Conference giveaways or souvenirs

When I open the envelope, they are shocked to discover that I have predicted at least 80 to 90 percent of the things they have come up with.

---

* The formal definition of 3-D printing: a process for making a component by depositing a first layer of a fluent porous material and then depositing a binder material; such steps are repeated as needed, until the unbound material is removed and a final product results.

Why am I able to predict so many of the ideas that my students come up with? One reason, they say, is because I have taught this class many times. But another reason is because we predictably focus on obvious opportunities—those that are driven by problems in search of solutions.

I then tell them to see the 3-D printer not in terms of problems, but as a reversal: a solution in search of problems. After all, I explain, a 3-D printer can create items to address hordes of problems out there. Inverting their perspective so that they see the power of taking an existing solution—such as the 3-D printer—helps them more fully understand the nature of problems. What would happen if we didn't start with an age-old problem but instead started with an innovative and unique solution and then retrofitted problems? Three-dimensional printing is an instantaneous, portable solution to manufacturing. When my students start with the unique assets of the solution, I get ideas like the following to solve more interesting problems:

Wire frames that can help prevent vineyard frost. Almost all winemakers struggle with vineyard frost. Freezing temperatures and frost pockets can severely damage vines and newly emerging buds. Most solutions are clumsy, like fans that try to pull warm air down to the vineyard floor, candles that give off enough heat to create air movement, wind machines, sprinklers, plows, and even helicopters. But it's possible to print a wire frame that stretches across the floor of the vineyard, providing a mechanism for evenly dispersed temperature.

DigiPuppets. Kids are obsessed with touch screens—how can parents and teachers turn screens into tools for productive play? My students had an idea to create touch-screen finger puppets for kids. These students actually did start this company; they launched with two lovable characters (Honey Bunny and Zip the Zebra) and four educational apps that are able to bring those characters to life while teaching important skills and life lessons.

Seeing problems in a different, non-incremental way allowed for atypical, unexpected connections and ideas. Indeed, one way to develop our ability to think exponentially and non-incrementally is to hone our ability to see where connections exist. But equally important to develop is the ability to see where connections do *not* exist.

The Narrative and the Numbers

In every situation we encounter, every industry, every company, every individual, there's a narrative and there are numbers. (Even when we are interacting with individuals, there are numbers and metrics, as we will see.) It's just that they're not always what they seem at first glance.

Let's start by looking at the narrative and the numbers in a company setting: the discount airline industry, for example. There are players such as Ryanair, Spirit Airlines, and Southwest Airlines.

Some of you who have taken Ryanair before are probably groaning out loud right now. I am. My experiences with this airline were downright painful. The seats were small, cramped, hard. My knees literally hit the seat in front of me—and I measure in at a cool five feet five. I remember one flight that I took from London to Dublin in which I had forgotten to print my boarding pass in advance, so they charged me an extra twenty pounds. The boarding process was like herding cattle.

With Ryanair, you wouldn't be surprised if they told you one day that you had to pay to use the on-board bathrooms. In fact, that is exactly what the airline experimented with a few years ago, charging people for the bathroom because the use of such a facility is a "luxury, not a necessity."

Not too long ago, I also heard the news that Ryanair was considering a standing room only section of the airplane so that they could fit more people into each aircraft. They discussed sections with bicycle-seat-style contraptions that would keep you in a standing, upright position, with a bar that would come down (like an amusement park roller coaster's) to keep you from jostling around while standing during the flight.

And then there's Southwest. To me, Southwest, though it's also a discount airline, has a markedly different feel. Flight attendants are helpful, happy, and downright hilarious. They make witty announcements, give food on the plane, and try to make flying an enjoyable experience. The boarding process is straightforward, and it's still free to check bags.

Southwest and Ryanair, while they are both discount airlines, have two distinct narratives on being a discount airline. For Ryanair, it's: Gosh darn it, when you are thinking about how to get from point A to point B and you want to do so as cheaply as possible, you're going to remember that Ryanair is cheap. They want you to *know* that they are a discount airline. They're cheap because they don't waste on frills like comfortable seats. Bad press around standing room seats and paying to use the bathroom—that's actually them purposely reminding you how very cheap they are. Ryanair encourages those articles about its no-frills experience. And when you want the cheapest flight possible, you happily pick them and then pat yourself on the back for remembering to print out your boarding pass in advance.

Southwest also reminds you that it is low-cost (though admittedly, not quite as low-cost as it once was). They also don't have the frills, but they emphasize all the things they do for you that are *free*: making it enjoyable, letting you check bags, letting you change flights when they have available seats. And why shouldn't they—these things cost them nothing, and hence cost you nothing. They remind you that they keep costs down but make your flight fun where it has no cost.

Their numbers? Nearly identical to Ryanair's. The financials are similar; the narratives make all the difference.

Lots of these types of differences in narratives exist. How you tie them back to the numbers and vice versa is where you begin to gain an eye for enriching. Finding the holes, the red herrings, is about looking for alignment between the narrative and the numbers. It's a great technique to look for areas where connections might *not* exist and where there may be incongruity. If it's a new lightsaber umbrella, it's about whether people will want it *and* whether they will pay for it—the narrative *and* the numbers. If it's a company like Juicero, the numbers (Will people pay for it?) are certainly a concern when you consider the narrative around what the product actually does. Was the addressable market that Juicero had identified accurate? Was it really every household in the United States? Every *single* household? Their narrative just didn't make sense. Their pricing didn't make sense. And the two vis-à-vis each other also didn't make sense.

The narrative and the numbers concept gives us a way to test our intuition about what might appear to fit but in fact is contradictory—in other words, it helps us fine-tune our gut feel about things that don't seem quite right. It allows us to predict and catch flaws, of the sort those early medical specialists did when thinking about Theranos, and those reporters did with Juicero. It's a technique that helps one to think smarter to gain that edge in ideas and innovation to enrich.

Making It All Make Sense

The narrative that Antje Danielson and Robin Chase, founders of the successful car-sharing company Zipcar, put forth was that people in large cities don't need to own cars; they don't need them on a daily basis. But people do find themselves needing a car on occasion: to get furniture at IKEA, to make a large grocery run, or to pick up a friend at the airport. So Zipcar allows access to one of their cars for the time period you need.

It's a compelling narrative, one that was fairly solidly in place at the outset, when Danielson and Chase first started presenting their company to investors in January 2000. But what allowed them to become what they are today was not the narrative. It was how the narrative meshed (or didn't mesh, as the case was) with the numbers they presented.

Looking at their earliest business plans, it was their numbers, and one number in particular, that a few astute individuals took note of. This number was their utilization rate. Zipcar had a proposed utilization rate of approximately 85 percent. This number presumably made sense—after all, Zipcar was using the rental car industry as a comparison, and most rental car companies had a similar utilization rate. But to those who thought a bit about it, an 85 percent utilization rate didn't actually make sense. This number didn't fit Zipcar's narrative.

What did the 85 percent represent? Well, if we think about it in terms of the number of hours in a day, what is actually happening during those twenty-four hours? What is happening during *all* of those hours, including between, say, two a.m. and six a.m.?

How many people do you think are looking for a Zipcar during those hours? How many people are looking to make that large grocery run, or drive to IKEA, or use a car at all? At an 85 percent utilization rate, it would mean that some people still want a car between two a.m. and six a.m., and furthermore, that all other hours outside that two a.m. to six a.m. time period are close to full capacity—100 percent utilization.

It just didn't make sense. For a rental car company, sure, you still pay for a longer-term rental car even when you're not actually driving it.

But that number just didn't align with Zipcar's narrative about folks needing a car in urban areas. Their narrative wasn't congruent with their numbers. Early investors passed and the company was almost never to be.

But the founders took note that their narrative wasn't congruent with the numbers—and that their numbers weren't congruent with the narrative. They understood that to make the company work, they needed to either change the narrative to fit the numbers, or tweak the numbers—even their growth projections, targets, and financials—to make them fit the narrative. And so they did, making shifts in how they thought about their fleet of cars, and in the reservation system, as well as adjusting their numbers and their financials. They finally arrived at a compelling case and the rest is history. Nowadays, you can find a Zipcar vehicle in almost every major city in the United States, as well as throughout Canada, France, Spain, and the UK.

• • •

It isn't easy to develop an intuition for noticing things that don't quite seem consistent. People are highly uncomfortable with what researchers call *cognitive dissonance*—when two things, be they beliefs, ideas, or values, feel contradictory. In fact, people find it so psychologically stressful that they reduce these feelings of uneasiness by actively avoiding or even changing the information to make it more harmonious.

Psychologist Leon Festinger found that human beings are basically hardwired to *not* notice things like inconsistencies between a narrative and the surrounding numbers. They change part of their cognition to eliminate the discomfort of cognitive dissonance by ignoring things that seem amiss and exaggerating the positives.

But if we engage in a conscious effort to seek out incongruities, we create opportunities to enrich. Learn to notice what's not there and to trust in what is there. Knowing the value you bring and trusting in your own perspective is the foundation of your edge. Then you can show others how you enrich. That's where we'll head next.

PRINCIPLE 5

Your powers of discernment come from trusting your intuition and your experiences.

PART 2

Delight

CHAPTER 6

The Power of the Unexpected

Everybody is a genius. But if you judge a fish by its ability to climb a tree, it will live its whole life believing that it is stupid.

—Albert Einstein

WHEN MY DAUGHTER WAS THREE OR FOUR YEARS OLD, SHE WAS, like many other little girls, obsessed with princesses. I have no idea how or why it happened, as I didn't say a word about princesses as she was growing, and in fact, I tried not to resort to typical gender associations at all.

Yet lo and behold, every night, as my husband got ready to read her a bedtime story and asked, "What would you like me to read tonight?" she would look at her bookshelf and ask, "Can we get some books about princesses?"

So my husband would say, "How about we read this book about Curious George, and then if you want, I'll tell you a special story about princesses that I made up all by myself?"

And so every night, my clever husband would invent a princess story—but not just any princess story, and not stories about princesses getting rescued by handsome princes or princesses with long blond hair who lived in beautiful castles. His princess stories were about Princess-Engineer Ashley, for example, who helped fix a technical problem in an engine when they were on their way to visit their grandmother, or Princess-Entrepreneur Kristin, who came up with a disruptive innovation that saved her brother's birthday party, or Princess-Chemist Amy, who used acids and bases to solve an important chemical problem, or Princess-Paleontologist Rachel, who not only learned the difference between paleontology and archaeology* but also made an important dinosaur discovery to boot.

Each princess was more than *just* a princess. Each princess was tied to an occupation, and each demonstrated some key character trait that was essential for success in life—be it grace under pressure, self-reliance, or patience.

My daughter fell in love with these stories—so much more so than she would have if they had just been about rescued princesses, and so much more so than if they had just been about a patient paleontologist or self-reliant chemist who shouldered responsibilities and was accountable for her actions.

Being authentic to her interests and finding a bridge to his own interests as an engineer and scientist allowed my husband to delight (and in turn enrich) in a pretty special way. It's a simple illustration of how you delight, and how delight leads you to enrich, but my daughter fell so in love with these stories that she started delighting her friends at school with her own versions of them. And when she grew old enough

---

* In case you're curious, paleontology is the study of fossils, while archaeology is the study of human artifacts and remains; paleontology deals with life in the past geologic setting, like animal and plant fossils, while archaeology is more focused on studying the remains of human beings and their past cultures.

to write, she started writing the stories down and drawing little sketches to accompany them.

Together, we have now written all the books, one by one, and turned them into a children's book series, called the Princess Heroes, that encourages girls to "be a princess *plus*." Many little girls love princesses. And that is completely okay. Yet rarely are princesses in stories made out to represent anything other than the stereotypical heroine, nor do their stories portray traits that will help with success in the real world. So our series was written to embrace many little girls' affinity for princesses, while also encouraging and emphasizing the skills that are shown to enable women to gain an edge as adults in the real world.

By figuring out how to interest my daughter, my husband made his message about strength and self-reliance resonate so much more than it would have otherwise. He knew how to enrich—but the delivery made all the difference.

Going from the Head to the Heart

In part one, we talked about how to enrich. But what is often overlooked is that we sometimes don't even have the opportunity to do so. Sometimes it is because we are written off and not given the opportunity. Sometimes it is because we aren't in the right social circles and aren't seen as belonging to the right groups.

Getting those opportunities comes through an ability to delight. When you know who you are and how you can enrich, you give yourself the confidence to delight the proverbial gatekeepers. By doing so you create the possibility to enrich.

Delight is the spark that allowed Elon Musk, if you recall from the introduction of this book, to let me in. I was set up to lose; I had no way to show how I could enrich. But delighting him catalyzed him to give me a chance and let me in.

My husband was already fully aware that our daughter loved princesses. What he wasn't aware of was that he was quite effectively practicing and cultivating the principles of delight.

> de·light /dəˈlīt/
> *verb* to give joy
> *noun* something that affords gratification

But delight is more than gratification. At the crux of delight is a component that most people miss: *surprise*. Delight is in the unexpected. In many ways, it's like humor.

Probing these similarities, I recently asked Hasan Minhaj how to be funny. Minhaj is an American stand-up comic, as well as a writer, political commentator, actor, and television host. (It may seem like an odd question, but in my defense, he had asked me an even more bizarre question first: "How do professors stay educated?" Amused, I retorted, "How do comedians stay funny?" And hence the start of a delightful alliance.)

What Minhaj told me surprised me. He said it's important for comedy to have a point. I had thought humor could and maybe should be pointless. But he continued by saying people should be authentic about the things they care about. When you use humor authentically, it opens the door to changing people's minds.

Logic and evidence are persuasive, but they can only take you so far. But a great joke can open doors wider. Psychologists Brad Bitterly, Alison Wood Brooks, and Maurice Schweitzer have shown that humor can be a powerful tool that allows you to manage impressions. In negotiations and interviews, your colleagues are more likely to view you as competent and attribute higher status to you if you can land a joke. And those jokes should be authentic and real, not contrived or cheap.

Humor makes people pay attention. "I've never told someone I'm Muslim and they're like, 'Cool,'" Minhaj said. But he went on to explain how he uses humor to note some observation he has about being Muslim, in a way that he can subtly change people's perceptions:

> We've only allowed eleven Syrian refugees into the US. There's more people on the playoff team for the Golden State Warriors than the number of Syrian refugees we've let in.

Or he'll comment on racism and equality for him as an American citizen, even though others don't always see him that way because of his skin color:

> My dad has a totally different view of racism than I do. To him, as an immigrant, he just sees racism as a "tax"—something like an "immigration tax." As immigrants, you endure racism, you endure discrimination—that's your tax.
>
> But *I* was born here. I'm just asking for what's on the receipt. . . . I price match, just like I do at Best Buy.

And then he can have a conversation and begin to enrich people's understanding of Islam in Syria, as the case may be, or his views on immigration policy.

Minhaj's theory of comedy is backed up by academic theory about humor. *Benign violation theory* suggests humor occurs only when three conditions are satisfied: (1) there is some type of violation, in that there's a disturbance, or something that deviates from or is counter to what is expected; (2) the situation is benign; and (3) both perceptions occur simultaneously. This explains why things sometimes *aren't* funny: a joke is lame and perceived to have been used before to the point of being cliché (i.e. it's so "obedient" that it's boring), or a joke seems overly aggressive or even offensive (i.e. it's not benign).

Delight is similar. When we delight, we violate perceptions, but in a benign way. Delight unsettles and challenges beliefs about your context, grabbing the attention of gatekeepers and making way for you to show how you enrich.

Delight isn't about trying to be charming, entertaining, or slick. But each of these attributes can tell us something about what delight *is*.

First, look for the unexpected. Practice seeing the peculiarities in everyday life, as I've hinted at in part one.

Don't overprepare. Go into situations in which you may face bias, failure, or disadvantage (whether real or imagined) with some prototypes and exemplars in mind that can provide you with the opportunities to delight, and that can place you in a position to enrich.

Remember that much of delighting is in situ, based on engaging with others authentically and in the moment. Use the existing context to hone your quick reflexes and help you with the delivery.

Seek out people, products, and situations that you yourself see as delightful. Try things out that you consider delightful, and consciously try to pinpoint what makes them delightful to you. Use this to help refine your own sense of delight and your own ability to delight. Use it to help you learn what is unexpected and, just as important, what feels inauthentic.

We all have the capacity to enrich. But when you are able to also delight, magic happens. That is how you encourage them to let you in to prove how you enrich.

Look How They Shine for You

Production of a movie called *Crazy Rich Asians* began in April 2017 in Singapore and Malaysia, helmed by director Jon M. Chu. It was a personal project for him. The story (based on Kevin Kwan's book of the same title) and its powerful message about assimilation and finding one's voice when stuck between two disparate cultures mirrored many of his own experiences as the son of a Chinese father and a Taiwanese mother raised in Palo Alto, California.

The movie boasted an all-Asian cast—the first major studio production to do so since *The Joy Luck Club* twenty-five years prior. But Chu didn't stop there. He was committed to underlining the cross-pollination between Asian and Asian-American cultures in all aspects of the film—including screenwriting, for which he hired Adele Lim, a Malaysian-American; and the food team, headed by Singapore chef and food consultant John See, who was tasked with capturing the flavors and colors of all the dishes featured in the movie.

And the same could be said of Chu's commitment to the music in his movie: he relentlessly tried to ensure that all the songs in *Crazy Rich Asians* captured, in his words, "that crazy blend of identities and cultures that makes up who we are." So he set out to find music that would blend American and Asian cultures, curating a list of classic Chinese love songs and popular English songs that could be reworked with Chinese lyrics and sung by Asian performers. Near the top of his list: a song by the band Coldplay called "Yellow."

Chu and his music supervisor, Gabe Hilfer, earmarked "Yellow" for the finale—the powerful song was perfect and hit all the emotional sentiments of the film's final crescendo; it just fit.

But when they reached out to the band, they refused.

You see, Coldplay had reason to be hesitant. In 2012, the band released a song called "Princess of China," accompanied by a video that featured Rihanna in traditional Chinese clothing. They were criticized for cultural appropriation and were slammed for their insensitivity toward Chinese customs. To make matters worse, they created a similar incident in 2016 when they shot the video for "Hymn for the Weekend" during the Hindu festival of Holi—with collaborator Beyoncé clothed in traditional dress. Audiences were outraged, and a prominent Hindu leader criticized the artists, saying the band treated their religion "frivolously."

Having already faced backlash for insensitively engaging with Asian culture, Coldplay understandably refused Chu's request to use their song in *Crazy Rich Asians*, citing the negative connotation the color yellow often has when applied to Asian culture, because of its demeaning attribution to Asian skin tones and color.

But Chu saw it differently. He had grown up a fan of Coldplay and loved the lyrics of the song. He wanted to use it to subvert the color's use as a racist slur toward Asians.

"[The word] has a connotation to it, from things that I've been called and culturally and all these things, so for me, it was more about ownership of that term," Chu said. "I remember hearing the song and the beauty of yellow, the color of yellow as the sun and of love. It was like, 'f— that,' because yellow can be beautiful, and if you're going to call me yellow then fine, that's what we'll be." Chu wanted to use the song to reclaim the word. "We're going to own that term," he said. "If we're going to be called yellow, we're going to make it beautiful."

So Chu didn't give up. Instead he wrote a personal letter to Coldplay members Chris Martin, Guy Berryman, Jonny Buckland, and Will Champion explaining why he needed to use "Yellow" in *Crazy Rich Asians*.

He began by outlining his "complicated relationship" with the color yellow, noting how the word had been used to disparage him as a child. But then he heard Coldplay's song. Chu wrote, "For the first time in my life, it described the color in the most beautiful, magical ways I had ever heard: the color of the stars, her skin, the love. It was an incredible image of attraction and aspiration that it made me rethink my own self image." He described how the song quickly became his and his friends' "anthem," helping them redeem the word *yellow* and making it something that they could take pride in.

Chu created a violation, unsettling the perspective that "Yellow" was offensive to Asians. He explained that he saw it differently—that he loved the song, he loved the lyrics—and that he wanted to *own* the color yellow. He simultaneously made his request benign and safe. Though he alluded to the racism that Coldplay had gotten accused of, he emphasized that he did not perceive it that way. His goal was to reclaim the term *yellow* and make it beautiful for Asians, rather than a racist slur against them.

Chu then segued into describing the film, proudly writing that it's about a woman "learning that she's good enough and deserves the world, no matter what she's been taught or how she's been treated, and ultimately that she can be proud of her mixed heritage." He explains that he envisioned "Yellow" playing as the character prepares to return home on "an empowering, emotional march"—a fitting anthem for a triumphant moment for the character, and for anyone like her or Chu himself who had ever struggled to reconcile their identity with an unwelcoming world.

He concluded by reassuring the band that the scene "will give a whole generation of Asian-Americans, and others, the same sense of pride I got when I heard your song . . . I want all of them to have an anthem that makes them feel as beautiful as your words and melody made me feel when I needed it most."

Within an hour of him writing to the band, they responded and agreed. They later watched the scene and were enthusiastically on board, allowing Chinese-American singer Katherine Ho to record a Mandarin version of the song. The song plays over the film's finale and climax—at the most poignant part of the film, just where Chu intended—when the protagonist realizes her own strength and owns her multiple cultures and identities.

• • •

Chu's letter delighted Coldplay, and showed how he could enrich. The inclusion of "Yellow" in the film gave Coldplay the chance to redirect their narrative: that they are a band sensitive to race, identity, and the nuance that exists in art and music and culture. The value this provided the band was enormous, given the negative associations they'd had to contend with. But they never would have recognized the value being presented to them had Chu not first delighted them, in turn disarming and making them accessible.

When you face critics, the ability to delight can create the opportunity to start afresh and provide you with the critical opening to show how you add value and how you can enrich. It can help you dislodge critics and subvert biases that others have against you. It can even help you make those biases work in your favor.

It's a lesson that I was taught early on by my parents, hammered in by a story I heard all through my childhood about my mother immigrating to the United States with twenty-two dollars in her pocket.

She had received an academic scholarship to study in the States, but while the scholarship covered her tuition, it did not cover a number of other things, such as books, room and board, and other living expenses. And like many immigrant stories go, my mother arrived with only some clothing, a few pictures, and the twenty-two dollars.

Upon landing, the first thing she did was look for a job, one that she could work part time between classes. It must have taken her a lot of effort, as someone who barely spoke English. But when my mother recounts this story, even today, she doesn't focus on how difficult it was. Instead, she quickly moves on to describing how she finally found the perfect job as a salesperson at a jewelry store. It was perfect in her eyes not because of the work she'd be doing, but because in addition to providing her with money, it came with an apartment to live in—*if* she was able to sell a certain amount of jewelry each month. That kind of incentive is exactly what my mother thrives on.

The owner of the jewelry store owned a number of apartments directly above the store. One of those apartments, a one-bedroom, was the one my mother lived in and shared with three other women—who became her best friends, and whom she still keeps in touch with to this day. They all worked incredibly hard selling jewelry, especially my mother. Every minute that she was not in class, she was trying to sell jewelry. She would keep the store open late into the night, hoping she would be able to get a customer.

But my mother quickly discovered that she did not have what it takes to meet her monthly quotas. Despite all her hard work, all her best efforts to learn about the jewelry business, she was not selling. Hard work alone was not going to help her meet that month's quota. No one was buying jewelry from a woman who spoke broken English.

So not knowing what to do, she decided to try doing the opposite of everything that she had done up until that point—as is her personality— just as a test to see what would happen. Whereas she used to eagerly approach customers as they came in the door, she now gave a nonchalant greeting. Whereas she used to assert her knowledge of gems, she joked with customers that she wasn't an expert in judging quality or rarity, but she was the best at knowing what was pretty and what was ugly.

A few weeks later, my mother became the top-selling jewelry salesperson in the store. She started to earn repeat customers, who would even bring their friends in to meet the "sassy, sarcastic jeweler."

My mother never mentions (and in fact refuses to address even when directly asked) the bias that she faced. But of course, she faced lots and lots of bias—as an immigrant, as an Asian woman, as someone who couldn't speak English perfectly.

She overcame this bias by using it in her favor. She violated the norms of what people expected from her as an Asian woman and a young employee. She replaced submissive and deferential with sassy and sarcastic. She did so in a benign fashion, becoming their partner and ally in purchasing decisions. All the while living rent-free in New York City for four years. The next chapters will explain how you can do the same (well, maybe not the rent-free part).

PRINCIPLE 6

Before people will let you in,
they need to be delighted.

CHAPTER 7

Reflective Improvisation

Before everything else, getting ready is the secret of success.

—Henry Ford

DELIGHT IS MOST DELIGHTFUL WHEN IT SEEMS ACCIDENTAL AND improvisational. But that doesn't mean it's purely impromptu. As you'll see, that is why it is so difficult to delight and create that edge—it's a careful balance between preparation and spontaneity, between not being ready at all and being overprepared.

This was none too apparent to a young French-Lebanese entrepreneur named Oussama Ammar when he began trying to raise money for a company he was starting, an intelligent crowdsourcing firm that connects global companies with a network of more than 950,000 experts across the world to solve their biggest R&D problems.

As he was based in Paris, he contacted dozens of investors throughout London, Paris, and Central Europe. But one particular investor caught his eye: a man who served as a director on a number of French energy and electricity companies, well known for his ability to develop young talent within his own businesses. He would not only be able to provide some of the capital they so desperately needed, but he could also help with strategy and business insight in many of the critical areas of the business.

But try as he might, all of Oussama's attempts to reach out to this investor failed. It seemed he just wasn't interested. Oussama knew that all he needed was another conversation with him—one in which he could fill in all the missing information that he hadn't had a chance to communicate in his initial encounter with the investor.

A few weeks later, Oussama's girlfriend came home to the apartment that they shared, mentioning a man who had tried to hit on her at a wine bar where she was having a few drinks with her friends after work. Trying to provoke some jealousy, she offhandedly remarked, "He even gave me his business card, and he's the president of some grand company." Oussama asked to see it.

When he looked at the card, the name was eerily familiar. "Call him and ask him to dinner," he said.

• • •

You can imagine that the investor was pretty surprised to arrive to pick up his date a few nights later and be greeted not by the enchanting woman he had met at the wine bar, but by Oussama. But after that initial surprise, he was charmed by the absurdity and humor of the situation. He and Oussama hit it off tremendously, and he became one of the most important investors in the start-up.

What Oussama credits with his success is his ability to be "nearly ready." Like Henry Ford, Oussama understood that getting ready is the secret to success. But what does getting ready mean?

To Oussama, it's being primed and prepared to delight when the need and opportunity arise. If you are prepared with the knowledge of how you enrich—and if you're sure that you will enrich once given the opportunity—you will have the confidence to be unapologetic and vulnerable, and to improvise when you see opportunities.

Oussama was unquestionably not who that investor would have expected when the door opened and he presented a bouquet of flowers to who he thought would be his dinner date. But in this instance, the surprise bred the capacity to delight, form a relationship, and mutually enrich. When we can look at the world through funky-colored lenses and experience the farcicality of situations, it ultimately provides fodder for our interactions with others and our ability to delight others.

Plan, but Don't Overplan

I personally learned about the improvisational nature of delighting others through one unforgettable incident. I was getting my master's degree at INSEAD, an international business school with campuses in Fontainebleau, France; Singapore; and Abu Dhabi. We were discussing a company that to this day remains one of the most bizarre companies I've ever heard of.

The company manufactured contact lenses for chickens. Yes, you read that correctly. Back in 1962, a farmer discovered quite by accident that some of his chickens were suffering from severe cataracts. As a result, these chickens were eating less. Not only that, they were easier to handle and got into far fewer fights.

Chickens are aggressive animals; they fight each other in all-out brawls that can be so severe that they often injure or even kill each other and then resort to cannibalism. Sometimes it's about establishing a pecking order, or turf wars when there is overcrowding, but other times, they might fight just because they are stressed or bored. The chickens suffering from poor eyesight were less likely to get into these skirmishes. Because they injured each other less, the partially blinded birds were far more profitable for the farmers than their fully sighted counterparts.

This insight gave rise to an idea. A company called Optical Distortion Inc. (ODI) had figured out a way to diminish the vision of chickens through contact lenses. (And not only that, they had developed a method for insertion and retention that would make the lenses simple and straightforward to use in chickens. Not an easy feat.) These lenses worked by reducing a chicken's field of vision and creating distortion—the chickens could still see, but the decreased vision prevented fighting and other unwanted behaviors. Moreover, the lenses were colored red; the developers didn't quite know why, but the red lenses further reduced violence and cannibalism in chickens who wore them. The lenses were more effective and more humane than debeaking and the other preventive measures being used by farmers, and required far less effort.

ODI was granted a patent for its lenses but also knew that bigger players in the agriculture industry would get around that patent in due time. So our class discussion turned to how the company could capitalize on the development of their product, and how they would handle their marketing and product rollout.

My professor, Ziv Carmon, asked me to play the role of ODI salesperson, and told me to give my sales pitch to my classmate Robert, whom he asked to play the role of farmer.

I was not prepared to give a sales pitch, so I was completely taken aback. But I had in front of me three bullet points about the case. Those three bullet points told me everything I needed to know about these ridiculous contact lenses designed to reduce chickens' eyesight. I had one bullet point related to the product, product features, and use cases.

I had one bullet point related to the financials. And I had one bullet point on risks, mitigants, and potential challenges.

Bobbing and weaving off of those three bullet points, I was able to present a sales pitch that sold even Robert—who had actually grown up in North Dakota and knew something about farming. When he asked, "Why would my chickens want contact lenses?" I responded with all the benefits to not just him but also his chickens. I treated both Robert and his chickens as the consumer and him as the customer. When he asked about the extra hassle, I was able to tell him, "Chickens who spend their days seeing red are truly happier birds, and farmers whose chickens see red are those who get to see black [i.e. numbers in the black, rather than numbers in the red] and are truly happier farmers." For every query, I had a smart response. And at the end of it, our professor quietly commented, "Damn . . . How did you get every one of us to want to shell out money for chicken contact lenses?"

• • •

What I learned was that the idea that you can never be too prepared is complete nonsense when you are trying to delight. Being prepared is a blessing. But being too prepared immobilizes you.

As Napoléon Bonaparte once said, "Over-preparation is the foe of inspiration." Overpreparation deprives us of the ability to bob and weave—to dynamically regulate and calibrate. We become slow-witted, dull, and inflexible. Martin Seligman's foundational research on preparedness has found that a sense of overpreparation can lead to worse results. It can lull people into complacency, leading doctors to overlook certain symptoms and clinical observations, resulting in misdiagnoses; and leading forecasters to miss predictions of earthquakes and other natural disasters.

Years after that class, I went on a real sales call. An entrepreneur I

knew named Todd had developed a stunning piece of accounting soft-
ware that could provide enormous value. But the customers he had
approached were all nos. Frustrated, he reached out to me to see if I
could help him sell it.

I spent a few weeks getting up to speed with the product and what
it could do, his cost structure and the features that he was still developing, and a few other details about the company and the services he
could offer. I went along with him to the next sales meeting, which was
with an interested customer based in the Pacific Northwest.

After a bit of conversation and banter, the customer assuredly
declared, "Great. I love it. I want to buy." I looked over at Todd and saw
the expression on his face turn to excitement and exhilaration, only to
be followed a few seconds later by a look of terror. Because immediately
after the customer said, "I want to buy," he asked, "How much is it?"

And Todd froze. Because *he did not know.* Now, you might think
he was an idiot for not knowing the price of his own product, but you
have to understand that this was a product that typically had required
long sales cycles (more than six months), involving numerous discussions about the features and capabilities, and finally, the price. Each
time Todd had met with a potential customer, there had been rounds
of feedback, iterating on the features, making improvements, tweak-
ing here and there. In addition, Todd had been immersed in the product design process for eighteen months, leaving him with little attention
to pay to pricing.

So after the momentary shock of realizing that Todd was not
going to respond at all and was in fact completely frozen, I pulled
myself together, reassumed an air of confidence, and said, "That'll be
ten thousand."

To which the customer replied, "Great, that's no problem."

To which I responded, "That's per year."

Which he followed with, "Sure, no problem."

To which I retorted, "That's per user."

To which he replied, "Oh, that's a problem."

And then I breathed a sigh of relief and we started to negotiate the price.

What prevented Todd from making sales, and what panicked him when his customer asked for a price, was too much information about his company. He was immobilized by his knowledge of all the product features, future offerings, services, and so on—so much so, he wasn't able to be flexible in thinking about ballpark prices. I had enough flexibility in knowing the price—I knew the *range* within which I could work. Yet we had to also know the company intimately enough so that we could legitimately talk about the product and what we could offer. It's a balancing act between being prepared and remaining flexible. Luckily, there are ways to develop and hone this.

A Repertoire of Prototypes and Exemplars

My daughter has been playing the violin for years, and recently a friend of mine commented on how wonderful that is. It's true, there are lots of benefits: playing an instrument is supposed to make you smarter, improve your concentration, your patience, your discipline . . . I could go on and on.

But I can confidently say (as my husband can attest*) that the primary reason that my daughter is still playing the violin is because I am

---

* He has commented multiple times how funny he finds it that I am so besotted with Tatiana. In fact, during arguments, he has been able to win me over to his side just by impersonating her to make me smile.

so smitten with her violin teacher, Tatiana. Tatiana is a superb violinist, yes, and fabulous at teaching my daughter the fundamentals of violin. But she is even better at teaching her the fundamentals of having an edge in life—though she's probably not even aware of it.

Tatiana teaches my daughter what to do when she is approaching a new piece of music, and by association, any new situation: "You must first think, 'Is this a march, a dance, or a song?'" You see, Tatiana explains, before starting any new piece of music, you must first identify whether it is a march requiring a strong, steady rhythm and a bold tone; a dance that brightly encourages listeners to get on their feet; or a song with irregularities and silences intended to mimic the human voice. If you don't know what you're playing, then you don't know what is expected. More important, you don't know what is unexpected.*

It's like what the truly remarkable Phil Anderson, one of the mentors to whom I am most indebted, once told me: "When you're asking a question, you should always surmise what answer you're expecting to receive back. Because otherwise, how do you know whether you are surprised or whether you've learned something?" Have something—anything—in your mind so that you know whether it is surprising.

And know whether what you're playing should sound like a march, a dance, or a song. It sounds trite, and obviously it's not just about a march, a dance, or a song. But it works in much the same way in practice. Take, for example, the students I work with on start-ups

---

* I could go on and on about Tatiana and her brilliant method—like how she is teaching my daughter confidence: "Are you a horse or a donkey? Because you are playing like you're a donkey. Please carry yourself like you're a majestic horse, and then people will see you as a majestic horse." Or how she is teaching my daughter about the importance of the fundamentals: "You must practice 'open bowing' every day. You must do it every day. It's like your medicine. It is the main thing in violin. Like your family is the main thing in your life."

and the entrepreneurs I coach who are seeking funding from investors. I tell them, "You must first think: Am I approaching them with a high-concept pitch, a two-sentence pitch, or an extended pitch?"

• • •

The *high-concept pitch*, the *two-sentence pitch*, and the *extended pitch*. Those are the prototypes that I tell them to think of and to try to assess. Whether it's actually a "pitch" or not—what approach are you going to take, which of those prototypes are going to be most suitable to make sure you delight so that you have the opening to enrich? What I did with Elon was totally a high-concept "pitch"—a one-liner. With Todd and the customer it was a two-sentence pitch—slightly extended, with a bit more detail. And selling contact lenses for chickens? That was definitely the extended pitch, with lots of back-and-forth and substantive exchanges of perspectives.

The high-concept pitch is really something that allows you to distill your point into three or four well-placed, poignant words. It delivers all the information your target audience will initially need, in a quick "shock." For example, if I were to ask you, "What is Facebook for professionals?" it would quickly get you to think LinkedIn. If I asked you about the all-electric Porsche, you'd likely think of Tesla.

But it's not just about companies. What is the high-concept pitch that you would want for yourself? Remember what I did to delight Elon: I stayed at the high level—I essentially provided him with a high-concept pitch—a quick bout of witticism that shrewdly alluded to his level of wealth.

Now contrast that with Todd's pitch. It was a bit more extensive and detailed (though the high-concept pitch can communicate a large amount of substance)—more of a two-sentence pitch (also referred to as an elevator pitch). This prototype is something I like to think of as how you distill a three-hundred-page business plan (antiquated, I know) into something easily remembered.

I teach my students that a two-sentence pitch might sound something like: For [target audience] who [has a need], the [product name] is a [product category] that [offers a key benefit]. Unlike [competitor or substitute], we [are different in a key way].

For example, Elon Musk might pitch Tesla like:

For *wealthy individuals and car fans* who *want a high-end sports car that is environmentally friendly*, the *Tesla Roadster* is an *electric car* that *delivers unprecedented performance without damaging the environment*. Unlike *Ferrari and Porsche*, we *offer amazing performance without any direct carbon emissions*.

What is *your* two-sentence pitch? And just as a start-up might have multiple two-sentence pitches—one for a supplier, one for a potential customer, one for a potential investor, and so on—what are your pitches and whom are they targeting? You're not going to delight your mother in the same way that you delight your boss; you're not going to delight your boss in the same way that you delight a customer.

And just as we saw with Todd and his customer, you're likely to get some dialogue going from a two-sentence pitch. You're likely to get some questions. That is the point. That is how you move from delight and start to enrich. What you should be doing during the two-sentence pitch is positioning yourself in such a way that it piques some interest in your counterpart and you elicit the types of questions that will allow you to shine and continue to delight just through your responses.

It's the same reason why I tell those I'm coaching, "It's not a pitch." When we think about pitching, we tend to equate it with selling—but it's really a conversation. You're trying to elicit interest and start a conversation.

And the same applies for that third prototype, the extended

pitch. And by extended, I mean anything that is longer than two sentences but shorter than one minute. No pitch should be longer than one minute—after that, you should be in full conversation mode.

Here are two real-life pitches that I present to students, one an example of what to do, and the other an example of what not to do. See if you can figure out which is which, and why.

Phil Libin, CEO of Evernote, in a pitch for his company:

Hi, I'm Phil Libin, the CEO of Evernote.

Evernote is your external brain—whenever anything important happens, you can put it into Evernote and you'll always have it on hand when you need it. You can use Evernote with lots of devices you currently have. We have a version for Windows and for the Mac. You can also use this from any web browser, any phone, or any camera.

Now, your memory can take many shapes—there are lots of things you will want to remember. So you can use Evernote, for example, to take a picture of someone's business card, or to take a picture of a whiteboard or a wine label that you want to remember. Or you can leave yourself a text note or a voice note— all this information goes up to the Evernote servers, where it's processed and indexed, letting you do things like search for all the texts in your images, letting you search by location. The information is then synchronized back down to your clients, so that it's always on hand so you can always find what you need wherever you are.

Everyone has two subscription levels: free subscription and premium subscription. Premium subscription is five bucks a month, and you get virtually unlimited storage and all sorts of other goodies.

And Rouzbeh Shahsavari, CEO of C-Crete Technologies, in a pitch for his company:

The most widely used manufactured material on the planet is concrete. On average, each person uses more than three tons of concrete a year. Unfortunately, the concrete manufacturing process contributes to more than 10 percent of carbon dioxide emissions worldwide.

However, we have been able to develop a concrete that not only cuts the carbon dioxide emissions by half, but also it is five times stronger than normal concrete. Our design is unique because we have discovered how to change the very nanostructure of concrete. This approach is environmentally friendly and at the same time it reduces the cost of concrete manufacturing by 40 percent. Given that the US market for concrete is over $100 billion a year, this makes our product extremely lucrative for concrete manufacturers.

We are a team of five researchers including three superstar professors at MIT. I myself—I am a last-year PhD student working on innovative concrete and we are looking for two more passionate people to complete our team.

There is only one focal thing that distinguishes these two pitches, really: the level of detail. The second pitch does a good job of staying on point and providing a few essential details. In the first pitch, however there are *too many details*. Anything longer than the two-sentence pitch—even if it's an extended pitch—should actually be thought of as having the same amount of content as a two-sentence pitch. The extended pitch situation is the one that we are most often going to be in. And when we think we have more time with an extended pitch, we end up saying things like: "You can take a picture of someone's business card, or take a picture of a whiteboard, or take a picture of a wine label ... You can use it from a web browser, or a phone, or a camera ... or your mother's camera, or your kid's phone, or your neighbor's phone. ..." You get the point.

We become enamored with all the features—all the things that we can do to *enrich*—when we haven't yet *delighted*. We think we have a lot more time with an extended pitch, but we should not be trying to fit any additional *content* into that extended pitch. All we are doing is providing more flavor and color. This is what the second pitch does well, and what the first pitch falls short on.

Three Talking Points

It doesn't matter which prototypes and exemplars you have in mind—it can be march, dance, or song; high-concept, two-sentence, or extended pitch; or any way that makes sense for *you* to frame a situation. Your prototypes can come in many forms. What's important is to have a few distinct prototypes and exemplars in mind, so you go into situations armed with an approach to take, while avoiding going in overprepared. You have freedom to modify and alter your message. You can fine-tune and calibrate as necessary. I couple that with a bullet point list of things to remember—the data, or facts—which can be paired with any of the prototypes, just as I did when I used those three bullet points on the contact lenses for chickens in class that day.

I find that three is all I can cognitively handle at one time, but you can use as many as you can adeptly manage at once. I do the same before important phone calls, where I'll take five minutes to jot down two or three bullet points; it's the right number to help me reflectively improvise in a way that creates cohesiveness and logical progression. It also helps me lead the conversation. By knowing the two or three things that are most critical or that the potential client wants an answer or resolution to, I'm able to steer the conversation—and again, reflectively improvise in a way that comes off as elegant, by making connections between topics in a way that is not tangential or random—and arrive back at these two or three things.

It helps me seem prepared and on top of things, and more than once, I have been told that people have been impressed with my poise and expertise. In cultivating a mind-set for reflective improvisation,* I am able to delight, and then impress, and finally enrich.

PRINCIPLE 7

Don't overplan. Instead, aim for flexibility and opportunities to delight.

---

* And speaking of reflective improvisation, in which one thing leads to another, leads to another, Ziv Carmon, that marketing professor who was leading us through the class discussion of the contact lenses for chickens, sent me an email after class that day, saying that he was looking for a research assistant and wanted to know if I was interested. Which led to me working with him, as well as another marketing professor named Jill Klein. Which led me to academia and my current work. Also in the class that day was a student named Chris Evdemon, who became a dear friend—the same dear friend who led me to the world of entrepreneurship and start-up investing, which led me to my work on edge. And Robert, the "farmer" who enthusiastically bought my contact lenses for his chickens, was Robert Dunnigan, who also became a great friend, and who led me to some of the most profound books that changed the way I thought about success, my work, and the importance of gaining an edge.

CHAPTER 8

Shaping and Delighting In Situ

Recognize the true nature of the world around you. Just like as if you were a plant . . . you have to know what kind of light situation you have. And the combination of plants [around you] is important, too, because some plants [always try to] take over the pot.

—Terry Izzo

THE ABILITY TO DELIGHT IS NOT ALWAYS SUDDEN AND INSTANTANEOUS— often it shows itself over a sustained period of time. Delighting frequently has to come in situ, drawing from a deeper understanding of the circumstances and backdrop of the position you find yourself in— or the place you're in.

It's what allowed me to recognize that Elon Musk saw Byron and me as two scrappy entrepreneurs trying to sell him a product. We gained a deeper understanding of what was going on within both Elon's mind and his companies at the time, and that allowed us to relate to him and capitalize on our time with him in an exclusive way once we captured his attention. It's what landed Sara Blakely, designer of Spanx, her first account—with Neiman Marcus, no less. Finding herself in the meeting where she was losing the buyer's attention, and knowing she had just one shot, Blakely immediately recognized the conditions underlying the buyer's criteria for purchases—she recognized the true nature of the world around her, her "light situation", as Terry Izzo says, and told the buyer to come with her to the bathroom. Blakely showed her the before and after versions of her wearing Spanx. It worked and the buyer was delighted with the brilliance of both the product and the pitch.

Understanding the circumstances and backdrop so that I could delight in situ knowing my own plant's "light situation", is what launched my career. One of the most significant periods in the life of an academic is going on the job market as a PhD candidate and doing your "fly-outs"—two-day visits at academic institutions interested in hiring you as a faculty member. Among the most exciting visits I did was, hands down, at the Wharton School, which wound up hiring me as an assistant professor a few months later.

But at the time, I didn't know that I would be offered a job, and hence should have been extremely stressed at the prospect. And yet, for some reason, I only felt a quiet calm—perhaps because I felt that Wharton was such a long shot for me anyway.

The centerpiece of fly-outs is a formal lecture that candidates give on their research, followed by a grilling by faculty. But the evening before my talk, I was to be taken to dinner. My hosts for this dinner were two of the senior faculty members in the department, Raffi and Mac. Both are revered scholars in the field; moreover, I had personally long admired (and been intimidated by) their work.

Raffi was to pick me up at the hotel I was staying at, and we would begin talking en route to dinner. Now, in my mind, I envisioned thoughtful, pointed questions about the rigor of my work, or deep conversations about the state of entrepreneurship research. Instead, as soon as Raffi picked me up, I could tell that we would be speaking more casually and freely. It was clear that I was going to like him—as much for his charm and personality as for his work. He started chatting with me about my family, Taiwan, and my childhood. We talked about the size of gas tanks and how I liked my steak. It was all as natural as if I were talking to an actual colleague, and I sensed that he was pleased with their choice to fly me out for a job talk. We got along spectacularly and I could tell he really wanted me to do well. At one point, he asked me, "What do you think your chances are here?"

To which I replied, "Honestly? Probably, like, three percent."

I was surprised that I had even gotten a fly-out. I had even asked my advisor, "Do you think it's just a joke that they invited me out? Like, they already flew out the four candidates that they really wanted, and then they were like, 'Hey, let's fly out the quirky girl who studies investor gut feel.'"

But Raffi, who seemed almost amused, didn't miss a beat, and replied, "I assure you, you have a much higher chance of getting a job here than that."

We arrived at the restaurant and the evening went on, with lots of conversation, with Mac asking me at one point to rate him on a scale of 1 to 5 on how trustworthy, likable, committed, and passionate he seemed (each of these a characteristic from my dissertation research that I had identified as impacting investors in their gut feel about an entrepreneur, so Mac's question wasn't nearly as random as it might seem at first glance). When I gave him a 3 for trustworthiness, followed by a 2 for likability, he roared with laughter.

I felt totally at ease with these two potential colleagues of mine. At the end of the evening, as Raffi dropped me back off at my hotel, he said to me, "You're a delight."

• • •

Delight is something you have to figure out as you go along, but it is built on a rich history and knowledge of what has come before. As we talked about in the previous chapter, having prototypes and exemplars in your mind can help, whether the type of delighting is quick and improvisational in nature, requires a bit more detail, or is sustained over time. During the dinner with Raffi and Mac, I was already familiar with their scholarly work and how foundational it was for the field of entrepreneurship—and I understood where my research fit in. I also had a tacit comprehension of the types of people they both ordinarily discussed scholarly literature with, and I saw how frequently they were approached at academic conferences by yes-men and sycophants seeking their approval.

When I dubbed Mac a 3 and a 2 on my scale, rather than all 5's as he presumably expected to hear, I bucked the trend, and furthermore gave him an opportunity to see me as an equal—a potential colleague— rather than as his junior. It provided the entrée for us to engage in an academic sparring of wits, in an area of research where I knew I had a commanding control. It both amused and delighted him, and it's a memory he tells me that, to this day, he still relishes. Rely on what you already know to help you make the most of the situational cues and chance opportunities you are given.

There Is Such a Thing as Indispensable

Before I was a professor, I was an engineer. Well, to be more accurate, before I was a professor, I was an investment banker, and before I was an investment banker, I was a consultant, and before I was a consultant, I was an engineer. In one of my first engineering jobs, I had a manager named Kathy Keller, who had been with the company for more than forty years. I once asked her why she had stayed with the company for so long, and she chuckled as she told me the story of how she only barely made it to three years.

Three years in, the company was going through a round of layoffs. She was one of the people on the list. They were told that they had two months, and would be given a two-month severance package starting that day. What they chose to do with those two months was up to them—they could continue coming to work, or they could take that time as personal time. Most of the people, understandably, decided to take the two months as personal time—some used it to travel; some buckled down and focused on finding their next job; others wanted time to rest and learn a new hobby.

Kathy? She kept going to work. Within days, she realized that because of all the employees who were now no longer at the company, the company was in short supply of people to actually do the work. As they looked for people to take on temporary assignments, Kathy offered. As committees were formed to try to figure out the succession plan going forward, as they looked for volunteers, Kathy stepped up. And as work was being redistributed, Kathy offered to take on as much as she could. "Why not?" she thought. "It's not like I was doing anything else, and searching for a new job was not taking up extensive amounts of time," she told me.

All these new roles that she took on gave her a distinct advantage: she created the opportunity to engage with and delight all the people who would remain in the organization—many of them senior managers and directors who were scrambling for talent.

You can probably guess what happened. At the end of the two-month period, she had multiple offers from senior leaders to stay. She had her hand in so many critical business needs that now depended on her. Not only had she managed to get to know and delight the senior managers who were in need, but her ability to enrich had also become indispensable.

Maybe Your Passion Is Cars, but It's Okay if It's Not

About a year ago, an acquaintance of mine, Erica, became a rep for a line of hair-care products that branded itself as luxury hair care, with "naturally based" products that promise to "nourish" hair. The company boasted a signature dry shampoo that promised to deliver "bounce and body."

At first it wasn't clear that Erica was a sales rep, as she didn't start out stating that she was offering any products for sale (in fact, I'm not sure she ever came right out and said it). Instead, what caught my attention was a series of strange Facebook Live videos that she broadcast. In each video, only about half was content—the other half was drivel, in which she would say things like "Thanks so much for joining!" and "Wow, Amber, so glad to see you on, hope your family is great," all throughout the video.

It was all so bizarre, yet enthralling. I began noticing regular comments from a number of people whose names I didn't recognize. And almost all the remarks were people talking about how beautiful her hair looked ("Your hair looks A-MA-zing!"; "Don't know what you're doing with your hair these days, but whatever it is, keep doing it . . . it is looking so healthy and beautiful").

It soon became clear that Erica and these commenters were participating in a multilevel-marketing shampoo business, with two goals: sell shampoo and get other people onto your sales team to sell shampoo through "inspirational" content.

I saw Erica *trying* to delight. But it was planned, it seemed simulated, and it was the opposite of delight. Delight is authentic. Delight comes from a place of honesty and sincerity because all it does is give you what was already warranted and deserved in the first place: an opportunity to show how you can enrich.

I cannot emphasize this enough. Delight is not flattery. It can be humor that gives you an opening to demonstrate the other ways you enrich. It can provide a softer landing for most of the bluntness that people erroneously use to get things done. It can be disarming. But it can't paper over shortcomings.

It came to a head when I saw Erica doing another Facebook Live video and she noticed a former high school classmate of ours watching the live stream, a guy who is known for loving muscle cars. As Erica started to talk about passion, she tried to delight by saying:

> Cars. Maybe your passion is cars. And you . . . whatever you do with cars, you're a car guru. Maybe you love taking apart the engine. You just love handling and tuning up cars. Maybe you like to do something with cars. I don't know . . . you know . . . soupin' them up. And you can't live without that passion.

There was no way Erica was going to convert that into showing any of us her ability to enrich. There are too many gurus out there talking about interactions with other people in a sales job. There are books and books about influence. But it's not about influence for the sake of influence.

You gain an edge when you take an authentic opportunity and

surprise people so that they leave with a pleasant feeling that allows you the opportunity to enrich and provide true value. People will remember how you delighted them—that's the "frosting"—but only because it's built on the foundation of some damn good cake. Frosting without the cake is too saccharine and doesn't stay pleasing for very long.

Reality, Sincerity, Authenticity

Authentically delighting in situ requires you to be constantly fine-tuning, as well as constantly attuned to how you can shape situations to present the opportunity for your talents and core competencies to become apparent.

In research I've conducted along with two exceptional women, Francesca Gino and Ovul Sezer, we've found that people overwhelmingly tend to cater to the interests, preferences, and expectations of others, rather than drawing from their own. This advice gets perpetuated a lot; we're told that people are more likely to like you when you ask them about their interests and talk about things that are relevant to those interests, and you allow people to talk about themselves. I don't disagree in principle, but the problem is that this guidance has become so pervasive that we can spot people trying to predict our preferences from a mile away.

Delight is *not* predictable. One of the reasons it gives you the upper hand is because you are able to surprise in a way that's simultaneously pleasing *and* unexpected. When we try to cater to others' interests, it puts them on guard.

This research demonstrates an even more dramatic negative effect when we contort ourselves to fit the interests, preferences, and expectations of others. Doing so negatively impacts outcomes because trying to anticipate and fulfill others' preferences increases our anxiety and feelings of inauthenticity, and creates an unease about actually being able to provide and sustain value later on. As a result, we are less able to interact with others in a natural way, and less able to riff on the comments of others.

Be okay with being authentic to your own thoughts and interests. Give yourself permission to demonstrate your own personality, and trust that your words and actions will delight even if they're at odds with another person's interests. We can delight only with our authentic selves, rather than hollowing ourselves out to please others.

• • •

It's especially difficult to resist catering to people when the stakes are high, like when you are trying to land a job. Year in and year out, I see the anxiety this elicits in hordes of students, many of whom end up receiving wonderful job offers right off the bat—but just as many start off discouraged by all the rejections they receive. I can tell you this, from years of observation: there is little correlation between those who receive the most coveted jobs and those who are actually the most deserving of those jobs.

Out of those who have bucked this trend, I have noticed one thing in common among them: in addition to being spectacularly bright and deserving, they seem to have a special capacity to delight—and the ability to do so authentically—so that they have the chance to show how bright and deserving they are. And in doing so, they gain an edge.

One such student, a woman named Antonia, stumbled upon a job that was exactly what she was looking for—head of business development for a health-care firm, a role that would provide her with the opportunity to learn, progress, and contribute to the organization.

However, when she went to interview for the position, she found out that the job required her to be based in Belgium or France, and she could only take a role on the East Coast of the United States.

When the interviewers asked her if that would be okay, she initially thought she should try to show her flexibility. After all, she had always been advised to say yes first and negotiate later. But then Antonia thought the company might appreciate her honest take on the role and its location. She says, "I engaged them in a dialogue about why the job location needed to be in Belgium or France, whereas all their growth and business development was poised to come from the US. They were surprised at first, but then looked really pleased with me and told me that I was right."

The company was so impressed with this unexpected argument that demonstrated why she would be valuable that they offered her the job on the spot—and promised that it would be based on the US East Coast.

The experience of another student of mine, Peter, also impeccably illustrates the power of delighting in situ, as well as his capacity to dynamically iterate in a way that allowed him to show his competence and dexterity. Peter was approached by a private equity company offering an internship—an extremely prestigious organization that everyone wanted to work for. After getting the offer, he found out that it was an unpaid internship.

So he reached out to one of the partners to inquire, and the partner quickly got to the point: "We have never paid our interns. At the end of the internship period, we make offers to those that are qualified, and our salaries and bonuses are within the highest quintile of all financial institutions. If the fact that this is an unpaid internship is a problem, there are dozens of qualified candidates for this internship who would gladly take your place, and we have never had a problem filling our intern class."

To which Peter replied, "People who work for free do shit work, and I don't do shit work. Therefore, I should be paid."

• • •

When we are in situ—in the midst of a particular context—we get a sense of our audience and how we can shape the conversation. Private equity has a distinct culture, one that Peter quickly became attuned to and used to his advantage. Had his discussion been a part of another field or industry, the way he envisioned his capacity to delight may have been entirely different.

But that day, with that particular partner, the partner was absolutely delighted. After hearing Peter's response, the partner paused for a few seconds, and then followed with thunderous laughter, saying, "You are going to fit in perfectly. You will be compensated adequately. I will see to it myself."

The takeaway is not that we should be brash and presumptuous. What worked for Peter that day was not audacity or arrogance—it was his ability to read the situation. He exhumed his preexisting knowledge about the importance of candor and sophisticated, polished delivery in the private equity industry, and was able to *authentically* delight by shaping the conversation in situ. Delighting others requires you to have an opinion or point of view—being authentic while having the audacity, or the stomach, you might say, to take a bold, surprising stance.

What Peter and Antonia both were able to do is delight by *looking for* the unexpected, and making the most of those incongruities. This is accomplished and appreciated by neophytes—as in the case of Peter and Antonia, to a certain degree—and experts alike. I once heard Michael Ovitz, the great talent agent who cofounded Creative Artists Agency (CAA) and then later served as president of the Walt Disney Company, describe delight as "the point where your brain and your stomach meet."

Aileen Lee, venture capital investor and founder of Cowboy Ventures, once described delight to me in a delightful way. Incidentally, she is best known for coining the term *unicorn* to describe those start-ups that are valued at a billion dollars or more (because, you know, "valued by public or private markets at over a billion dollars but less than ten years old" is a cumbersome thing to say). Aileen is similarly eloquent when she describes how she invests. She looks for brands she calls magical—"new services that are delightful, and product-oriented founders who create magical experiences for customers"—companies that delight her.

She spoke about Uber in this way, describing the first time she was picked up in an Uber as a "magical" experience. "Uber certainly felt like that—once you started doing it, you were still thinking, 'Wow that was so cool, it was so easy, it made me feel so special.'"

It's about feeling special, and the additional effort or money that you're willing to put out because of it: "The Starbucks-ification. Like, coffee used to be ninety-nine cents, and now you're willing to pay three or four dollars for it because it makes you feel so much better. It's like a little treat during the day."

How do you recognize something magical and delightful? Seek out people, products, and situations that you yourself see as delightful, and consciously try to pinpoint what makes them delightful to you. Aileen honed her sense of what's delightful, both in companies she invests in and in herself. The more you do so, the more it helps you refine your own sense of delight and your own ability to delight. I've seen many people successfully do this to help them learn what is unexpected and, just as important, what feels inauthentic.

We all have the capacity to enrich. But when you are able to also delight, that is where the real magic happens. That is how you allow them to let you in, and how you build your edge.

PRINCIPLE 8

Stay authentic and embrace
how delight occurs in situ.

PART 3

Guide

CHAPTER 9

All the Ways Your Diamond Sparkles

You never realize how much of your background is sewn into the lining of your clothes.

—Tom Wolfe

WHAT DO YOU DO ONCE YOU'VE BEEN LET IN? ONCE YOU'VE shown how you can enrich, through first delighting others? The answer seems clear: you just enrich. You do the work. And yes, it's true—to a point. But not only do you need to do the work, you also need to guide how others perceive your work and your worth.

> *guide* /gīd/
> to direct, to steer; to influence the course of action

We need to guide because the levers that enable success are often outside our control. And those who pull the levers are making judgments and decisions based on their perceptions of our competence and character.

We can't demand that others pull the levers, but it's within our power to direct *how* they pull the levers. We have the ability to guide the course rather than settle for the course of action that others decide for us.

That's what this next part of the book is about: how you guide others' perceptions of you and how you can enrich. It won't be easy and it's certainly complicated. But it is essential that you better understand your inner workings and the "lining" of your "clothes", as Tom Wolfe says, for those external clothes to serve you well when others see them. You *must* guide that process; otherwise those preconceived notions that others will have about you—and they will exist, whether they are benign or malicious—will guide in your place. And in doing so, you can use the biases that others have against you in your favor.

Guiding, Following, and Knowing Yourself

Be yourself. This is a piece of advice that we've all heard, and most likely given to others. I've said it many times. A friend is about to interview for a job and they are nervous. What do I say to them? Be yourself. Someone is giving a big presentation? Just be yourself. About to ask someone out on a date? What do people say? Again, just be yourself.

This advice is great in principle, given the benefits we derive from delighting others authentically. But it doesn't give very much explanation. Without understanding the nuance of "being yourself," it can be very dangerous. It doesn't work for everyone. It's complicated.

When people say, "Be yourself," we tend to think first about what we are good at. Sometimes it's something that people can put a clear label on and communicate easily to others—"I'm good at tennis; I was invited to the junior Olympics, and am ranked sixteenth in women's singles," or "I play piano, and I played at Carnegie Hall at the age of ten."

Other people, like me, have a harder time describing what we are good at. When I was younger, the best I could do was to say that I was good at school. I loved school, especially math; when I grew up, I wanted to be a math teacher. I took pride in memorizing my multiplication tables, I loved the elegant way that solutions to long-division problems fit into neat columns, and I loved the symmetry required to solve algebra problems. Math came naturally to me.

A large majority of you are probably shaking your heads vehemently, either silently horrified or silently mocking me and secretly hating me. But I didn't have an advantage in many other things. I was small and timid; I was last in line for just about everything else. This was one of the only areas I had identified where I had a natural advantage. And even then, it was something that I recognized as an advantage only after I encountered it as a bias that people might hold against me.

. . .

My sophomore year in high school, I had Mr. Heine for algebra II and trigonometry. And then I had him again for precalculus my junior year. (I'm a product of public schools. Not a huge budget for teachers, you know? So I tended to have the same teachers for multiple years.)

In the beginning, I *adored* Mr. Heine—truly worshipped the man. Mr. Heine also loved math. He loved it so much that he would squeal in delight when he drew a perfect parabola on the board. I learned a ton from him—about math, as well as about having an edge. Or the lack thereof.

Mr. Heine had a "perfect test" bulletin board. It was prominently displayed at the front of the classroom, hugging the blackboard. If you got 100 percent on a test—it had to be a test, not a quiz or a homework assignment—Mr. Heine would write your name on a gold star and display it on the board for the *entire year*. Now, this wasn't just any gold star—this was the mother of all gold stars. This was a ten-inch star that

Mr. Heine would meticulously cover in thick, shiny, gold-colored paper, with perfect edges. And then he would carefully apply vinyl lettering, with your name and the date of your perfect test, precisely centered and aligned on the gold star. It was truly beautiful to behold. And what made these gold stars so desirable is that they were scarce. It would be a surprise if Mr. Heine handed out more than five or six in any given year.

Over the multiple years that I had Mr. Heine for math, guess how many gold stars I got. Zero.

Now, that probably would have stung regardless, but what made it particularly upsetting to the fourteen-year-old version of myself was that there was another girl in my class, Elizabeth, who got nine gold stars over the course of those two years. Not to take anything away from Elizabeth, because she was probably damn smart. But I do remember looking at her test papers on each of the occasions that she got a perfect 100 (the test papers were proudly displayed next to the gold stars)—and observing that our tests always looked nearly identical. On each of those occasions, when I may have gotten a 99, I'd notice that she'd have written something like $7x = 49$; $x = 49/7 = 7/1 = 7$. I, on the other hand, might have written something like $7x = 49$; $x = 49/7 = 7$. I'd get a point taken off for not showing my work and including 7/1.

When I tried to ask him questions about why I got points taken off, he would tell me that each time I questioned his grading, he would take another point off. I stopped asking. I also stopped asking questions in class. I noticed that when Elizabeth was struggling with a concept, we would spend days on that topic, and I would become agonizingly bored. When I would ask for clarification, he would tell me that he couldn't stop the entire class to explain, and that I should ask a friend to help explain it to me outside class.

At the end of that year, to be allowed into honors calculus for our senior year (rather than basic calculus), we needed to have a teacher sign a form. I remember sleepless nights, worried that Mr. Heine wouldn't sign my form, even though I had gotten close to 100 on nearly all my tests. When I finally asked him to sign my form, he looked at me and said, "I don't think you're ready for honors calculus." He signed the form for many others in the class, students who I knew struggled with math.

After that, I decided I no longer wanted to be a math teacher. I decided I was no longer good at math.

Self-Awareness Encumbers Our Ability to Guide

Self-awareness is a sense of who we are, what we value, and what our inherent strengths are. When we say "self-awareness," we mean knowledge of who we are internally. But gaining an edge requires knowledge of your inner self *and* how it interacts with the outer world. It's both within you and contextual. That's what I didn't yet understand.

We need to own who we are *and* the context—what is within us and what is around us need to complement each other in order for us to be successful. I didn't understand that self-knowledge and self-awareness only go so far if you ignore the truth of others' perceptions and don't take control to guide them.

As far back as 1890, the philosopher and psychologist William James spoke about self-awareness as a source of continuity that provided an individual with a sense of "connectedness" and "unbrokenness." As researchers gained more clarity and confidence into the construct, self-awareness came to be defined as the capacity for introspection and recognition of our own values, passions, aspirations, and interactions with our environment.

These early definitions, however, emphasized the self, rather than the social self. And modern-day examinations of self-awareness seem to do the same. Self-awareness has become the latest buzzword, with everyone trying to become more self-aware—as the popularity of BuzzFeed quizzes can attest. (Which episode of *Friends* best matches your personality? Which Disney princess are you? What city are you? What color best describes your personality? I'll admit to doing at least a couple of these.)

Science has its own version of these quizzes—for example, the widely used Myers-Briggs Type Indicator (MBTI). The MBTI attempts to inventory your traits and place you into one of sixteen personality "types," capturing all your attitudes and preferences (Are you more introverted or extroverted? Do you function more through thinking or feeling? Sensing or intuiting?) into one parsimonious label.

I'm the first to admit that I find tests like the MBTI to be a fun way for me to categorize and be more aware of my own values, feelings, and motives, and provide a context to talk to others about theirs.* But tests like this are problematic† for all sorts of reasons. Many do not meet the basic criteria of psychometric scales. In fact, tests like the MBTI lack general external validity, are based on outdated psychoanalytic ideas, and dangerously oversimplify to the point where they are no longer scientifically and methodologically accurate. In addition to methodological concerns, we should be wary of all these tests because they create the illusion that our "selves" can stand independent from externalities.

We use tests like the MBTI and often take them as gospel. But this popular conception of self-awareness doesn't really account for contextual and interpersonal differences. This is detrimental to truly gaining a sense of self-awareness because personality is a continuum rather than a series

---

* I'm an ISFJ, for example, and while we're on the subject, my husband is an ENTP, the complete counterpoint. Which makes things interesting, let me tell you. Often when we have a disagreement, I am quick to point out that he should stop being such a "thinker" and try to be more of a "feeler." It has never worked. Not once.

† (even outside of marriage)

of binaries. While I might tend to be introverted, in actuality, I'm some-where between introversion and extroversion depending on the context. We're all somewhere in between depending on the context.

Assessments like the MBTI assume static personality traits, when in fact the most successful people perceive their personalities and skills as fluid and are able to represent themselves differently and adaptively.* And therefore it's damaging for us to think of our "selves" as static and monolithic because we may be missing out on opportunities and occa-sions in which we might have an advantage. When we neglect to pay attention to how context affects our personality, we also limit our ability to find and cultivate our edge based on the situation at hand.

What we want is to balance who we are with the external environ-ment in a way that is additive, rather than limiting, so that we can, as Judy Garland once said, "be a first-rate version of ourselves, instead of a second-rate version of somebody else."

• • •

We've been focusing on other people's perceptions of us and how that informs our view of ourselves. What happens when we experience an internal conflict? How do we accommodate what others tell us we should be, while simultaneously gaining clarity and precision in defin-ing this sense of self *and* guiding external perceptions of that self?

---

* And even if we look at other, more validated models of personality, it behooves us to remember that personality traits are on a continuum. If we assume one can score high, medium, or low on any single dimension of personality, then we have 243 (3^5) different types of people in this world that we are trying to influence and adapt to! That's only looking at the "big five" personality traits—if we look at the BFAS 10 aspect model of personality, we get 59,049 (3^{10}) personality types. Or, as my friend, psychologist Scott Barry Kaufman, pointed out, if we want to get really crazy, we can assess ourselves using the AB5C model of personality, which has forty-five total fac-ets of personality. That gives us 2,954,312,706,550,833,698,643 personality types.

Most of us begin with a strong sense of internal self-awareness—a sense of who we are, what we value, what our inherent strengths are—before it is shaped by what others tell us about who we are, what we value, and what our strengths should be. As a student, I was intuitively aware that I was good at math. I would just absorb mathematical concepts, and it was something that was fun for me. It made me feel light, relaxed, and carefree.

But our natural awareness is chipped away as we become attuned to the opinions of others. We live in a loud world, one where we are interconnected to others, whether we choose to be or not. What we are able to achieve and how far we are able to go is often in the hands of others—managers who determine promotions, investors who determine the financial resources we'll have at our disposal, partner organizations who determine our place in the market, and yes, math teachers who determine our future career trajectories. It is inevitable that we will be affected by how other people view us, and how they perceive us when we are merely trying to "be ourselves."

We might think one way to cope is to ignore the perceptions of others—to silence the things around us so that we can hear our own voice. I'm certainly an advocate of mindfulness and meditation and understand how this provides abundant benefits—but it cannot be the entire solution. The reality is that we do operate in a world of interdependency. It's impossible to isolate yourself from others' opinions and ideas. Those who seek to rely only on their own voice and their own silence quickly find that it is not sustainable.

But it is also not about allowing the interactions and perceptions of others to define who we are without our input, without individual agency, lest we allow others to dictate our own values, feelings, motives, and desires. We allow others to damage us, just like I allowed Mr. Heine to impact how I perceived myself.

Instead, we have the power to guide how we position ourselves to others and hence how others perceive us—but first we need to understand our "self": the perceptions we have of ourselves, and how we internalize others' perceptions. Only then can we take an active role in guiding and reconciling the voices, opinions, and perceptions of others vis-à-vis who we know ourselves to be.

The path forward—the path to creating an edge for oneself—is therefore about acknowledging and receiving the perceptions of others, while simultaneously empowering yourself not to embrace and adopt those views. You can accept the perceptions of others so that you can consciously address them and confront them—but without embracing and internalizing them. For as we'll discuss later, the views of others are overwhelmingly not about you at all—they're about their own insecurities, their own goals, and their attempts to reconcile their own sense of self-awareness.

Were my fourteen-year-old self privy to this, I would have recognized how Mr. Heine's perception of my skills affected my own self-perception. And that might have shielded me.*

You're Not Selling Out When You Reclaim an Awareness of Your Self

In Newark, New Jersey, Ashley Edwards knows how to talk the right talk. Her father grew up in the inner city of Newark, and a large proportion of her family still calls it home. To her, it's also a hometown,

---

* But it's funny how things work. I have to say, in all sincerity, that Mr. Heine was truly the best math teacher I have ever had. And I will be grateful to him until the end of my days, for what he taught me.

the city where she spends most of her time. She cofounded a tech non-profit called MindRight to empower Newark youth of color to heal from the type of trauma—such as emotionally abusive relationships, neglect, and physical violence—that she observed and encountered in her own childhood.

Ashley is in her element at MindRight, talking twists and goddess braids with students while also helping them deal with the aftermath of seeing classmates being shot dead or dealing with parents being incarcerated. It's often tough, but as a black woman, Ashley feels like she belongs. It is her home.

And yet her home at one time was Palo Alto, California, one of the highest-earning towns in the United States, where she attended Stanford University for her MBA. Before that, New Haven, Connecticut, where she attended Yale University and majored in economics. But the amazing memories she holds of Stanford and Yale are also interspersed with poignant memories of the struggles she faced and the feeling that the advantages those prestigious universities promised to bestow were for others, not for her. She remembers classmates who were offered financial funding from professors to start ventures for "ideas that were based on nothing." Those offers were never even an option she considered available to her as she sought funding for MindRight.

Getting people to take her and her nonprofit seriously was a struggle from the beginning. She launched MindRight while at Stanford and approached investors at philanthropic foundations who financed ventures just like hers. She thought it would be a perfect fit, and maybe it was—but *she* wasn't.

At first, investors told her to "come back to us after you've won more fellowship awards" so that "you can show us that you're a serious contender." She told herself that investors just wanted to know she had the credibility to do it (and tried to stifle any other thoughts, even as all around her, nonblack peers and friends from Stanford and Yale were being lauded as credible, talented individuals coming from prestigious institutions). Despite her degrees, she felt like she needed to prove herself over and over again because of the color of her skin. It made her resent the privilege of her top-tier education, and it made her frustrated and angry.

When she began to win prestigious fellowships—the very fellowships that had been cited by those investors a few months prior—she was told that she needed to "do a pilot first, so that you can get more data and can demonstrate more credibility." After three successful pilots in Camden, New Jersey; Washington, DC; and Newark, where she was able to demonstrate not only a viable business model but also that they were already earning revenue, the message shifted yet again. This time, it was simply that they were sorry that they could not invest.

She eventually bumped into these same investors at panel discussions at various conferences and events, where she would listen to them talk about their commitment to equality and funding people of color. She heard how they were lauded for their commitment to diversity and inclusion, and how they were considered game changers in a new, inclusive social entrepreneurship ecosystem.

Ashley remembers the day she reclaimed an awareness of her "self." She was in a meeting with another potential funder when, completely unrelated to her organization, he began to talk about Burning Man, the annual event at Black Rock City, a temporary city erected in the deserts of northwest Nevada where people come together to celebrate the arts, self-expression, civic responsibility, and decommodification, among other things. She played along. When he started comparing Burning Man to other festivals such as Coachella and Cannes, she continued to play along. At one point, the conversation felt surreal to her; the contrast between this conversation and those she'd been having with her students just an hour prior was stark.

She realized that her students in inner-city Newark would have no idea what Burning Man was—and yet *she* could carry on a scintillating conversation with opinions about this festival, and about Coachella and Cannes. These were places, cultural references, and topics that were also a part of her makeup—things that she had a perspective on and an understanding of, because of her time in top-tier institutions. She could talk this talk as well.

Rather than fighting to prove and reclaim her status as a highly educated minority woman from an "atypical" home city, Ashley decided to start owning her background and perspective. Funders, she realized, were partially driven by a lack of understanding of what trauma in Newark looked like. They had preconceived beliefs about who she, as a black woman advocating for mental health in inner cities, was and should be. And she realized that it was "crazy that I had allowed people to make me feel like it was about me—and not about them."

She started doing all her initial interactions with investors over the phone—where investors could not tell by the sound of her voice that she was a black woman, and where she could connect with them based on her education and apparent privilege.

She gave herself permission to embrace both identities, carrying her Yale backpack to meetings with investors and not letting herself entertain any feelings of selling out her Newark family—she had earned her Yale identity just like anyone else there had.

She found that this was the most difficult part for her—feeling like she was selling out. But it wasn't selling out. It was giving herself permission to embrace all the varied and complicated pieces that made her, well, *her.* Once she allowed herself to reveal all the facets of her experiences, even vulnerably discussing her trials with depression and mental health with investors, it allowed her to guide investors to a different level of understanding of MindRight. She showed that she was the rare person who intimately understood both the community Mind-Right served and the objectives and motivations of the investors who funded it.

Ashley realized that by embracing who she was—all her identities, her multiple selves—she was able to cultivate an edge for herself, which allowed her to associate more effectively with others in both worlds and show how she could enrich. As Ashley describes, "It helped me flow in these worlds. In both worlds. I felt like I was flowing, rather than being halted."

• • •

"Being yourself" requires embracing all the varied and complicated pieces of yourself. For Ashley, embracing all her identities collectively gave her an edge. But for others, that may not be feasible, and external demands may force you in directions otherwise. People have expectations for how you "should" be.

Self-awareness, in fact, is made up of two components: internal self-awareness and external self-awareness. And these are inextricably linked. As William James wrote, "A man has as many social selves as there are individuals who recognize him and carry an image of him in their mind." We come to know ourselves by observing how we fit into the fabric of social relationships and what others expect of us.

There are many versions of ourselves. And there are many versions of who others expect us to be. But with true self-awareness, you can guide others and the perceptions of others nonetheless.

One for Me and One for Them: Guiding the Expectations of Others

In the early 2010s, Ashton Kutcher starred in a number of movies. One was the dramatic biopic *Jobs*, in which Kutcher played the visionary Apple founder Steve Jobs. Another was the outlandish romantic comedy *Killers*, in which he played a goofy assassin turned good guy.

Kutcher was strongly advised not to take the role of Steve Jobs, for fear that it would negatively impact his career—a successful career that he had built playing the down-to-earth romantic protagonist.

A few months after *Jobs* was released, I met Kutcher at a conference. An audience member asked a question about the impact that actors could have in the world, and his response surprised me.

I'll admit that I never expected to quote Ashton Kutcher in my entire life, but what he said that day has continued to resonate with me, and it is something that I have repeated many times when people struggle with trying to "be yourself" in the midst of societal and external pressures, demands, and realities. What he said was this: "I do one for them, and one for me."

What he meant by this is that it is important to balance and consider external demands of who others want you to be while also giving yourself the freedom to embrace the realities of your personal choices. He has to decide what movies to do. His agent puts pressure on him to do certain movies. For a long time, he was seen as someone best suited to romantic comedies, movies in which it was assumed that his charm would sell tickets and bring in large audiences.

But what he wanted to do was artistic movies, things that spoke to him personally—theater productions, artistic and indie films. Films like *Jobs*. But he also knew that in order to survive and be successful in

Hollywood he needed to maintain his audience and his relevance, by doing those chick flicks.

So how did he describe what he does? "I do one for them, and one for me." One film that gets him the audience and maintains his celebrity. And then one that really speaks to him personally.

Some might see this as selling out. But I see it as an artist smartly guiding expectations and finding a way to thrive within others' expectations. We are complicated creatures, with multiple identities. There may be some identities that are more salient in some situations than in others, but they are still very uniquely ours. Kutcher is both a rom-com lead and a critically acclaimed actor in ambitious films. He gave himself permission to own all his strengths, including the ones that weren't as personally fulfilling but still served a purpose. When we have that kind of self-awareness, that's when we can guide others without compromising our own ambitions and desires.

* * *

And so how do we get a strong sense of our self (while not excluding the external factors that we must depend on)?

As we've seen from many of the experiences of others described in this chapter, when we tell people to "be yourself," it is confusing. There are so many versions of others. There are so many versions of ourselves. So first, compare yourself with yourself, not with others.

Second, remember that life rhymes. Look out for what rhymes in your life—the situations that seem to repeat themselves, the similarities in both your successes and your obstacles.

Third, as you begin to pick up on these patterns, don't go for absolutes; go for directionality. We tend to want to package, in a neat little parcel, the sum of who we are. But it's enough to just identify what areas are your "right directions" and which are your "wrong directions." It's actually better that way.

Going for directionality, rather than absolutes, helps you manage the impressions of others and guide their perceptions. You can be more fluid and adaptive, and you don't have to try to guess at what exactly they want you to be (because as we saw, they don't really know). You can embrace and bundle multiple identities, like Ashley Edwards was able to, or disaggregate and separate multiple identities while still owning them all, as Ashton Kutcher described doing. It gives you permission to be all the glorious versions of yourself.

If you go for general directionality, you'll be more likely to avoid striving for goals that don't leverage your strengths and that make it harder for you to create unfair advantages. Too often, we pigeonhole ourselves into what we think our strengths are, rather than building on those strengths. Rather than saying, "I'm an athletic person, so I'm going to try lots of sports," we force ourselves into one particular sport that we are going to excel at no matter what. What we sometimes fail to remember is that we are not one-dimensional beings. Self-awareness, in and of itself, is an elusive goal. We never really know ourselves; the best we can do is find general directionality.

And finally, going for directionality allows you to simply move toward something that feels right, while already finding ways to cultivate an edge. Just start going toward something—don't worry about if you haven't yet found *the* direction. When you go in that direction, do you feel light, free, and happy? Or do you feel fearful, constricted, and dark? Is it a situation or an interaction that makes you feel this way? Rule out some of those, and your choices become clearer. Sometimes the easiest way to figure out your right direction is to know which ones are the wrong directions. And keep yourself moving in the right direction without limiting yourself.

Often, having a vague direction in mind leads to multiple opportunities for success rather than one chance to avoid failure. Your success is rarely dictated by one single outcome that constitutes the *W* on the win column. There are lots of different ways to win. That's what we forget. We see one path that worked for someone else, and then try to replicate that, forgetting that there are infinite ways to get from point A to point B. And there are lots of point B's.

For Kutcher, it was giving himself permission to embrace what would delight and enrich others, as well as what would delight and enrich himself.

For Ashley, it was about her ability to feel like she belonged when she was with students and community partners in inner-city Newark, but also simultaneously giving herself permission to embrace how she belonged and could be a part of the Yale and Stanford elite.

· · ·

As for me, eventually I did find my way back to math. Even though I decided that I no longer wanted to be a high school math teacher, I never stopped loving math.

The next year, I had an amazing chemistry teacher named Mr. Kost, who encouraged me to go to college, and to major in engineering. I did, and I did.

But even as I studied to be an engineer, I recognized that I was a different type of engineer than other people, and was taught to recognize how *I* would have to guide.

Part of the difference was my gender. I remember electrical engineering professors talking about current by stating that many of us must have tried to stick our fingers into electrical outlets as kids, and remarking to myself that it was probably something boys usually did because girls were dissuaded from doing so, like I had been.

Part of it was my lack of experience and my lack of familiarity with and access to computers. I also remember a professor talking about processors and assuming that everyone had tried to take apart a computer at some point—and thinking about how I had never had a computer of my own, let alone taken one apart. In those days, computers were only something rich kids had at home—the only ones I had seen were the ones I got to use once a week in computer lab.

Given all this, it probably shouldn't have been surprising that I found engineering to be extremely hard. Damn hard. So hard that I failed my first test in my very first engineering class, a computer science class, with a score of 37. Out of 100.

I quickly realized that I was probably going to lose my scholarship, but then two things happened.

First, I called my dad and told him that I wasn't smart enough, and that I needed to switch majors. But he gave me a piece of advice that I still give my own students. He gave me permission to switch—as soon as I could tell him what major I would switch to and why I would like it better.

I couldn't conjure up another major. He helped me realize that too often we derail ourselves from a path before we've even had time to refine it. When things are going badly, lots of different options look better. But if we think about it and try to visualize what even one of those other options might look like in reality, we realize they might be very much the same, or even inferior.

Second, my computer science professor, a wonderful woman named Dr. Laura Bottomley, called me into her office the next day after class. I thought she was going to tell me that I was going to fail the class and that I should drop engineering. But when I got there, she had a copy of my exam in her hands and asked me to explain my solution—in words, not in code—and to explain my thinking. And I did. She did the same for the next question and then the next. And then she paused and said, "You know exactly what you're doing—you just don't know the right syntax." She gave me a C.

She asked me if I had ever done any programming before, if I had ever seen any programs. I told her that I'd taken a typing class in high school. She asked if I had a computer. I said no. She asked me about open lab hours at the computer cluster. By then I was choking back tears as I explained that open lab hours were at the same time as my work-study job.

She nodded, and then told me something that I've never forgotten: that she too had nearly failed her first engineering class, but that there is no right way or wrong way to do this; there is no one-size-fits-all. That I was headed in the right direction, and I should give myself the chance to go in that direction while embracing who I am and how I think about the world.

She told me that I may not have had the opportunities that others have had, and may never have those opportunities—but that I did have something. And that we are all diamonds; we are all diamonds that sparkle in different ways.

• • •

Self-awareness is like a diamond, sparkling differently from every angle. There are many facets of a diamond, and sometimes the light will hit at one particular angle, and other times it will hit at another angle—and sometimes it will hit multiple facets at once and appear spectacularly brilliant.

Cultivating your edge is about knowing each of your own facets and knowing how they will shine to those who are looking. There is no right or wrong way. Too often, even when people have a strong sense of self, they don't use it. The advice to "be yourself" actually limits us from doing exactly that. There isn't one singular version of oneself. There may be flaws and you may have disadvantages, but you have a diamond. And you can guide how your diamond is perceived, you can delight and differentiate, and you have the power to enrich.

PRINCIPLE 9

"Being yourself" entails guiding others to all the glorious versions of yourself.

CHAPTER 10

Turning Biases and Stereotypes in Your Favor

People hear me through their eyes first.   .

—Author unknown

CHRISSY TEIGEN, A SUPERMODEL WHO HAS GRACED THE COVER of *Sports Illustrated* numerous times, has had to address, time and time again, critics who slam her for being "too fat." She has told many stories about how that word—*fat*—has defined people's perceptions of her. One of the most vivid stories is of the time she was fired in the middle of a photo shoot for a major clothing company, in front of dozens of photographers, directors, and executives, because she was . . . "too fat."

But as time went on, and after being fat-shamed one too many times, Teigen decided that *she* would be the one to guide the message about her weight. She was going to own her own identity, rather than letting others create it for her.

On one occasion, she posted a picture on Instagram of her bare stomach, clearly showing her stretch marks, with the caption "mom bod alert!"

On another, she saw a tweet from her good friend Kim Kardashian West, who tweeted a full-frontal picture of her body covered in a plaster cast, writing, "We took a mold of my body and made it a perfume bottle @KKWFRAGRANCE."

Owning her own body weight, and not to be outdone, Chrissy promptly retorted: "well I'm going to put out a COMPETING PERFUME from a mold of my giant body and it will hold TWICE as much perfume as your bottle and the people will get MORE perfume."

Chrissy Teigen is not *just* a supermodel. Yes, this woman has graced the covers of *Vogue*, *Cosmopolitan*, and *Glamour*, but she is also the author of bestselling cookbooks and has her own line of kitchen products as well as beauty products. Oh, and she's also married to John Legend and raising two young children. She clearly works hard, maintaining her career, her family, and her figure. And yet, she tweets about how "large" she is (never mind that she was about six months pregnant at the time).

She knows she has her haters. And she knows the perceptions that they have of her. Some have called her attention seeking, some have criticized how publicly she shares news of her family, and some just see her as too fat.

But rather than going along with those stereotypes, or even trying to ignore them, she embraces them. She uses the stereotypes to guide people to the point that *she* wants them to make. About her role as a model *and* a mom. About how her self-image extends beyond her weight. About owning all her identities and allowing herself to be gloriously all her. She is a supermodel, but she can be a supermodel in her own way: as wife of John Legend, as mother to Luna and Miles, and as an independent person who tries her hardest to remain down-to-earth.

• • •

Perceptions matter. They certainly matter in modeling, even though the industry is evolving and embracing more positivity and inclusivity. But they matter even in our everyday lives, even as we strive for more equitable systems and a more inclusive culture.

Chrissy Teigen will always need to acknowledge that there will be stereotypes that people hold about models—that they must be skinny. Just like I'll always need to acknowledge that there are stereotypes that I will face as an Asian woman. Not too long ago, for example, I was setting up slides in my classroom, getting ready to teach a new MBA course, when a student mistook me for the IT support specialist who was ostensibly setting up for the professor. Easy mistake, right? Asian woman equals tech support, not professor.

Stereotypes invade our interactions. A couple of nights after that, I was having dinner with a rather diverse group of friends. As I relayed the story to them about how I had been mistaken for the person setting up for the professor, rather than being the professor, it was amazing how quickly our conversation spiraled to stereotypes in general. "As a black woman, I'm angry and aggressive. But as a black man, I'm seen as violent if I'm aggressive—and I'm good at sports, to the point where I'm dumb and can't think about anything else."

The racial stereotypes came fast and furious: Asians are dorky and meek; Latinos are loud, hot-tempered, and volatile; blacks are aggressive, outspoken, and threatening. So too did the gender stereotypes: men are messy and disorganized; women aren't smart and their place is in the home.

Then we got to cultural stereotypes: Americans are obese, lazy, and dim-witted; the British are rich and snobby; Italians are in the mob; Russians are angry and love vodka; Nigerians are dangerous; Bahamians are on the beach all day with coconut bras and no internet; South Koreans are always taking selfies; Singaporeans get thrown in jail if they chew gum.

There are even more stereotypes about class: the upper class are well-dressed, intellectually superior, posh, and well spoken; the middle class are white collar, live in suburbia, and are obsessed with owning their own homes and cars; the working class are blue collar, factory workers, with little savings.

And let's not forget some of the others out there, lest we leave anyone out: politicians are philanderers and only think about personal gain and their own benefit; librarians are old and boring; blondes are dumb; old people are out of touch; teenagers are rebels; bankers are sexist and greedy; and people who work in tech are geeks.

Have I managed to offend just about everyone now? Okay, good. Here's why this matters. Everyone has something. We are all susceptible to stereotype and judgment no matter who we are. Classic research on social perception tells us that we all rely on stereotypes to some extent. Psychologists Mahzarin Banaji and Brian Nosek have shown how the information and observations that we pick up from people's physical appearance, facial expressions, tone of voice, hand gestures, and even body positions or movements are used to form impactful impressions of, and large-scale inferences about, other people. We have limits to our cognitive capacity, our working memory, and the mental effort we can exert—and so we rely on inferences about a person based on observations of their behaviors or on secondhand information to help us out.

In doing so, we must acknowledge that all those around us do the same, and so we all fall prey to being categorized in certain ways, even disadvantaged, as others try to process the limited amount of data that they can process at any one given time.

What if we could take that "burden" off others? What if we could lessen that cognitive load? What if, rather than expecting others to rely on stereotypes, we helped them see what we want them to see?

We can do this by simultaneously recognizing the unfair judgments while guiding them instead to what we *want* them to see in us. Guide them to the attributions that you want them to make about you rather than being a bystander in the attributions that others are making about you. Having a strong sense of self-awareness and an awareness of how others perceive us also helps us understand the expectations of others so that we can better associate with them in a way that provides an advantage, rather than just trying to aimlessly fit with the external context by engaging in unfocused self-enhancement.

We can do this, and we should. But we often don't. We bemoan the unfair judgments that others have about us—and complain about bias. Bias does exist, and it's incredibly frustrating. But rather than beating our heads against the wall, we can empower ourselves to do something about it. We can flip things a bit in our favor. We can use the biases that others have against us in our favor.

This is such a critical point that I want to repeat it: if you guide the perceptions of others, you won't have to be at the mercy of their stereotypes.

• • •

When Cyrus Habib decided to run for lieutenant governor of Washington, he knew it wasn't going to be easy. He knew that he was not the stereotypical political candidate—someone who is tall, polished, and charismatic. Cyrus is rather short, coarse in demeanor, and blind. Not the picture of a successful public figure.

But he also knew that winning the election wouldn't be the hardest thing he had ever done, nor would it be his greatest achievement if he won. Cyrus, an Iranian immigrant, was already a Rhodes Scholar, a Truman Scholar, and a Soros Fellow. He had studied at Columbia University and the University of Oxford, and received his law degree from Yale Law School, where he served in the prestigious role of editor of the *Yale Law Journal*. And don't forget, he achieved this all fully blind, having lost his eyesight at the age of eight.

Cyrus was four months old when he was diagnosed with retinoblastoma, and by the age of two, he had lost sight in one of his eyes. Over the next few years, the vision in his healthy eye continued to deteriorate until doctors were forced to remove his retina when he was eight years old.

When he first told me his story, I have to admit that I was overcome with sadness and regret—what could he have done had he not been blind? I felt guilty thinking this way, and when I shared this with Cyrus, he showed me his amazing ability to guide others' perceptions. He assured me that sadness and compassion is exactly what he expected me to feel. It's exactly what most people feel.

He went on to share how he doesn't think of his loss of vision as a loss; he experienced sight for long enough to retain memories of visual images of the world. Cyrus considers it a blessing that he became blind young enough to still have the time to adapt and learn how to live a normal life without sight.

Hearing his story reminds me that he indeed has lived a normal life thus far, and he continues to strive to live a normal life. In fact, he has achieved more in his thirty-eight years than most—in spite of his disability. And listening to Cyrus speak, I realized that his challenge hasn't been the blindness itself. Cyrus doesn't talk about overcoming disability, but about overcoming bias—through self-awareness about his disability and others' perceptions about his abilities.

When Cyrus was in third grade, he was told that he couldn't play on the playground with the other children during recess. Instead, a teacher would have him sit by her side while the other children climbed on the jungle gyms and scaled the recess equipment. He was told that it was because teachers were worried about his safety, and they probably actually were. But it was also a form of bias, one that he didn't quite know how to understand at that age. Angry and frustrated, he would repeatedly try to explain that he was fine, that he could manage. The response was always that it was too dangerous.

That became the norm, not just on the playground, but in situations that Cyrus continued to face, time and time again: borrowing books at the library, taking karate lessons, learning to play the piano. Over and over, people assumed that he would fail or be incapable before he even had the opportunity to try—and the disadvantage was real even though it was rooted not in hate or fear, but in pity and compassion. The same compassion that I felt hearing his story. The same bias that I was guilty of because of the lowered expectations I might have implicitly had for Cyrus due to not wanting to oppress him, or not wanting to burden him with more than I (not he) thought he could handle.

Cyrus the third grader began to spend evenings and weekends on the playground with his mother, learning the lay of the land and where there might be obstacles or sharp edges on the playground equipment. He did the same upon arriving in New York City, when he had to figure out the Port Authority Bus Terminal. And again at Oxford, learning the layout of the campus and figuring out how to maneuver around the city. He learned to navigate physical spaces. In doing so, he also learned how to navigate his encounters with others.

When Cyrus first decided that he was going to run for lieutenant governor and began to tell his friends and supporters of his intent, he already knew what their hang-ups were going to be, what criticisms they would offer, and what doubts they would express. He already knew how he could preempt those doubts. He had long known that as he walked alongside people, allowing them to physically guide him because of his handicap, as he hooked his arm onto those of colleagues, of friends, he was also literally guiding them—by sharing his perspective. When people started expressing their doubts and tried to nudge him not to run, he was prepared. When people said things to him like "Running this type of campaign involves so much door-to-door interaction with people; it involves so much canvassing. Is this going to be too much for someone with your condition? Are you going to be able to navigate?" he was prepared. He recognized that it came from a place of concern. He understood that they wanted to support him and to ensure his safety, but they were so worried about his limitations that they couldn't see his strengths.

Cyrus's response?

I ask them if they have ever heard of a place called the Port Authority Terminal in New York City. And I remind them that I had learned to navigate the Port Authority Bus Terminal. I explain that I went from "Braille to Yale." That I had somehow navigated thousand-year-old dorms and cobblestone streets when I was at Oxford. Navigating neighborhoods, going door-to-door, I'm sure I can find a way. It's not the hardest thing I'll ever have navigated.

And navigate Cyrus did. He canvassed door-to-door. He connected with voters. He used his awareness of his disability to guide voters the same way he had guided his friends and mentors into understanding his ambition and turned them into supportive constituents.

Cyrus owned his disabilities and his limitations as part of his self—because they *are* part of his self. But how he has dealt with his limitations, and how those limitations were overcome and will continue to be overcome—that's the advantage that he can communicate. That's how he has always been able to turn a bias that others have against him to work in his favor.

Cyrus ultimately won the election to become lieutenant governor of Washington. As he did with voters, he quickly established himself as a self-aware, attentive politician. He uses that awareness to guide different perspectives and people of different walks of life so that they can come together and discuss issues that matter.

"I take the opportunity to walk with them," he said. "That creates a bond and reminds us that we're really all going to the same place. I guide them away from who they think I should be, to who I am." And that has allowed Cyrus to not only contend with his disability and the disadvantages he may face because of it, but extend his disability into an edge.

Stop, Drop, and Redirect

Paul Graham, who cofounded Y Combinator, one of the most influential start-up accelerators and seed capital firms in the world, once said, "One quality that's a really bad indication is a CEO with a strong foreign accent." He went on to say that it's difficult to communicate if you have a strong accent and that "anyone with half a brain would realize you're going to be more successful if you speak idiomatic English, so they must just be clueless if they haven't gotten rid of their strong accent."

After facing severe backlash for his comments, Graham elaborated on his stance to say that a big part of running a successful company is being able to sell it and accurately communicate your mission to others. An accent might hinder communication.

On the heels of his comments, I decided to study this stereotype about foreign accents. And what I found was that in the United States, people with nonstandard accents (i.e. Russian, Japanese, etc.) were much less likely to be promoted to middle- and upper-management positions.

The most common assumption for why this might be so? Stereotypes that people with nonstandard accents were not able to communicate as well—like Graham's assumption. I decided to test this. In a research experiment, I had people randomly assigned to listen to a message delivered by either someone with a foreign accent or someone with a standard American accent, and found that there was *no difference* in what they understood. I asked them to recall facts and details from the message they had heard, and there was no difference at all in what information they gathered.

Digging a bit deeper, my colleagues and I found something more surprising. Those decision makers, who were determining promotions, knew that they could not (openly) discriminate based on things like gender, race, ethnicity, and in this case, accent. But it was widely accepted that things like interpersonal influence, being a team player, and "thinking outside the box" were all attributes that everyone could agree were important. And it just so happened that every single person with a foreign accent scored lower on those things—which in turn led to them being the least likely to get promoted to management positions.

When it came to our findings of entrepreneurs with a foreign accent, again, there was no difference in terms of what they were able to communicate, but those with an accent scored lower on ability to influence others, a key criterion that all the investors could agree was important for the founder of a start-up. And in turn, their likelihood of securing start-up capital was much lower.

But our most fascinating discovery was that even though those with a non-native accent were less likely to get promoted to leadership positions, and entrepreneurs with non-native accents were less likely to get funding—in both cases because they were deemed less "interpersonally skilled"—there were ways for individuals to preempt those perceptions. Recognizing that others would form judgments about them based on their accent, they could redirect misattributions about their competence to give themselves an advantage.

To illustrate: When Emmett, one of our candidates in a job interview, said, "I know it might seem like I'm not able to communicate impactfully, but let me tell you about a time when I fought for resources for my team . . ." this individual was actually rated higher than those with no accent. When Nien Qi, one of our entrepreneurs, mentioned how she was able to "politically navigate a crowded supplier market in order to receive preferential pricing terms," she redirected the perceptions that investors had of her and obtained far more funding than her counterparts.

The "disadvantaged" person acknowledges the misattribution in a nonreactive way, linking it to a specific qualification and asset that they bring to the table. Numerous studies have found that addressing implicit bias and stereotypes directly, however, is not always the best way to reduce disparities.* When bias is confronted directly, it often leads to backlash in the form of increased prejudice and discrimination.

---

* For instance, if a candidate were too say, "Don't assume I'm bad at engineering just because I'm a woman." Or if someone were to say, "You think I'm a bad driver? Is it because I'm Asian?" I may or may not have uncouthly said both of these things at some point in my life.

Psychologists Alexander Czopp, Margo Monteith, and Aimee Mark even found that confrontations not only increased the hostility of the person being confronted but also created negative self-directed, internalized emotions in the confronter.

Focusing on behavioral change and structural interventions that may not require you to address bias specifically sometimes gets you much further. Put simply, what we showed is that we are capable of guiding and redirecting others. We can address any preconceived links—stereotypes—that people are making and break that linkage to form a new one.

As Charlie Munger once said, "Recognize and adapt to the true nature of the world around you; don't expect it to adapt to you." Once you have a pulse on how others tend to see you, you no longer have to rely entirely on their perceptions of you; you can guide them to how you want them to see you.

• • •

When Dawn Fitzpatrick started her career as a twenty-two-year-old at the American Stock Exchange, traders made bets on how long she would last. She understood that it was a manifestation of their insecurity about how long *they* would last. When they questioned her confidence, she recognized that it was about *their* confidence. When they questioned her about her ability to take risks, she recognized that it was rooted in their aversion to risk. So she created her own playing field and set her own standards, no longer tying herself to what was dictated or established by her male coworkers' norms.

As she was beginning her career at the investment bank UBS, she kept a pair of Christian Louboutin shoes under her desk, but often walked around the office barefoot as a display of her confidence—separate from other people's conceptions of what confidence should look like. When they questioned her ability to make tough decisions and pull the trigger on risky investments, she refused to play their game. She stepped away from "testosterone battles" and displays of dominance, gains, and competitive success. Instead, she created a position that started from a place where risk was about humility and having the insight to cut losses more quickly. "I communicated [my] belief that 'women have more ... humility in their investments ... [and will] cut losers quicker, in a more effective way than generally men will,'" so that she could guide and demonstrate her positioning.

"Clearly, there are single moments in time when I would have rather been a 6-foot-3 blond-haired ex-football-playing guy. But those tended to be offset by the times when I thought it was an advantage to be a woman," she once said. "I guided people to those advantages," reiterated Fitzpatrick, now one of Wall Street's most powerful women, running a $26 billion fund as the chief investment officer of Soros Fund Management.

In my research and in the research of many experts in the field, we find that guiding others requires an understanding of how others think of you on two key dimensions: (1) power and status differences, and (2) cooperative or competitive interdependence. Power and status differences are relatively straightforward to explain. They merely refer to how others see themselves compared to you in the social hierarchy. It's not a bad thing or a good thing; it's just a determination that is a fundamental element of social life, and one that emerges spontaneously to help coordinate interpersonal dynamics. But the greater the power differential between you and another, or your organization and another organization, the more you need to be attuned to the cooperative or competitive interdependence that might exist between the two of you.

In these cases, the more you can anticipate the needs of your counterpart, and in turn align your needs with their goals, the more you are able to guide in a way that allows you to be nonreactive and show how you can enrich and bring value.

Even in cases where there may be no power differential at all, however, cooperative and competitive dynamics still ensue. *Cooperative interdependence* and *competitive interdependence* refer to assessments of whether the other person is someone you expect to cooperate with or compete with. This determination also colors the dynamic. For example, imagine you are interviewing a candidate for a job in your organization. Do you expect the candidate to be someone you will cooperate with, or derive benefits from? Or do you expect that the candidate will compete with you in some area of your work? If it's the former, you may discriminate in their favor; if it's the latter, you may discriminate against them.

What does this mean in normal language? "When we're in harmony, but distinctly different, that's when magic happens," the gifted pianist Ji-Yong Kim said. Be together, but not the same.

These determinations matter because they impact how you will guide your interaction. The reason Dawn Fitzpatrick was able to endear herself to her coworkers is because she was able to level the power and status differences (or at least make them seem irrelevant), while forming a sense of cooperative interdependence. She saw that her colleagues perceived her, as a woman, to be competing with them on a different dimension and by different definitions of confidence and risk. To mitigate this, and as you now know, she very cleverly helped guide and redirect their perceptions of her.

• • •

The next time I was set to teach a new MBA course, I made sure to preemptively prepare to be seen as the professor and not as the IT support specialist. I proactively did some reconnaissance by speaking with current and former students and colleagues, and I discovered some of the common perceptions and attributions that my students had of me—namely, that I didn't "fit" their perceptions of what a professor should look like—I was too young and too female.

And so I helped redirect their judgments. I started out the class by saying, "I know it may look like I'm here to sell you Girl Scout cookies," redirecting them away from my youth and my femininity to my credentials,* quickly establishing what would ultimately be the tone of the class.

Later in the week, I did much of the same when I was scheduled to interview a venture capitalist for some research that I was doing. We met in his office, and I excitedly saw that he had an autographed basketball on his shelf, with signatures from Patrick Ewing, John Starks, Charles Oakley, and numerous others from a New York Knicks team of yore. As a huge Knicks fan, watching almost every game growing up, I commented on it, and was met with a look of derision. I quickly discerned that his assumption was that I, as a young, Asian female, couldn't possibly know anything about his beloved Knicks.

I stopped and redirected the conversation. We started chatting about my background as an engineer (yup, that fit, Asian engineer), and my prior experience working with VCs in my research, and I was soon on solid footing again. Once I had established that, I started making offhand connections between what we were discussing and random statistics and facts that I knew about the Knicks ("Yeah, you made

---

* All the while being careful not to take it too far, lest it backfire and students think I was overly self-conscious about negative perceptions. I didn't want to give the impression of "trying too hard," so to speak.

that deal work. Sometimes you just need some Anthony Mason kind of brute force behind you to enforce your position, am I right?"), which began to amuse him and even impress him.

To guide and redirect, I needed to start with stereotypes—the baseline of me as an Asian female and the behaviors he was expecting from an Asian female. And then I used those stereotypes to provide just a little twist, something that allowed me to redirect. This investor provided me with all the information that I had hoped to gain from that meeting, and when I left, he promised me two courtside tickets to a home game of my choice at Madison Square Garden to see the Knicks.

Use the biases and stereotypes that others have of you in your favor. Guide them to the attributions that *you* want them to make.

PRINCIPLE 10

Know how others see you, so you can redirect them to how they *should* see you.

CHAPTER 11

Framing Perceptions and Attributions *Your* Way

Your mission isn't your guide. You have to find your own way.

—Yellow Tanabe

DECIPHERING HOW OTHERS SEE US IS SOMETIMES LIKE PUTTING together a jigsaw puzzle: we have only a vague notion of what the overall picture looks like at first, but clarity and specificity come as pieces start to come together. But what makes it even more imprecise is that each time we interact with someone new, it's a new puzzle image.

It's like going on a diet, really. A couple of years ago, I decided to go on the Paleo diet, which you may have heard of or even done yourself, because it was all the rage for a while. A friend of mine, Anna, was raving about how it was changing her life. She was seeing amazing results. Like, incredibly obnoxious results. I tried to be happy for her each time I heard her say something like "The pounds are literally just melting off!"

Now, this is a friend of mine who has never been known for her willpower, someone who had tried every diet in the books and was never able to stay on any of them, and yet she was exclaiming how happy she was and how amazing she felt. And so I tried to cheer her on. And then I decided that if Anna could do it, I could too.

And for a while, I actually did do it. I had to avoid many foods, including but not limited to sugar, oatmeal and other grains, and processed food in general. Those things took a few days to get used to, but it was manageable. The hardest part for me was cutting out dairy, as I have a love affair with cheese—but I made do because the diet lets you eat lots of meat (bacon, even!), and oil is totally fine.

The first week, I felt like crap, but Anna reminded me that feeling like crap the first week means that the diet is working. (Apparently it's a real thing. People call it the "Paleo flu" because the first week you feel tired, sick, and sluggish, as if you really have the flu.) But then I started seeing some results. I lost a few pounds (not as many as Anna, but still . . .).

And it became easier. I started to get used to eating only eggs at breakfast. I incorporated almond butter and nuts into my regular repertoire, and even got accustomed to putting my meatballs and pasta sauce on top of spaghetti squash instead of actual pasta.

Three, four, five weeks passed. And I started talking about how this was no longer a diet, but a lifestyle (yes, I was one of those annoying people). But then, about six weeks into the Paleo diet, something happened. I had an allergic reaction. Like, a nightmare of an allergic reaction. Rash, swelling, blisters all over my face, especially around my mouth.

What I discovered is that there are different body types based on different genetic makeups (but of course). With different body types come different dietary needs, one of which is called an arginine-lysine balance (lysine and arginine are two amino acids found in protein-rich foods). Though I am not allergic to nuts, when I have too many, it throws my arginine-lysine balance out of whack and I find myself highly deficient in lysine. Apparently, I actually *need* lots of dairy. Like, *lots and lots* of cheese.

What did I learn? Not every diet is suited for every body type. Just because the Paleo diet forbade cheese didn't mean that I could, or should, stop myself from eating plenty of it. I couldn't commit to a strict Paleo diet. As yellow Tanabe safely advises, I had to adapt and find my own way to engage in this "mission" of mine. And, more philosophically, there are an infinite number of people in this world, all of whom need and want different things. Creating your edge in any situation requires a personal perspective and personalization. We have to find our own paths, not just follow the paths that others have made.

• • •

Not only are there infinitely different people, we often forget that we are dealing with imperfect creatures who are themselves fickle, people who might hold multiple expectations of others simultaneously. This especially applies to those who are in positions of power and are making decisions on behalf of others. We tend to think people generally agree and that there is a universal norm surrounding beliefs and perceptions that we can follow.

But that is far from true. The people we depend on to make important decisions that alter the progression of our lives don't know what they are looking for or how they make their decisions, and even when they claim to know what they are looking for, the target shifts from instance to instance.

Over the past ten years, I have met and interviewed more than 500 entrepreneurs and 350 investors. I often ask entrepreneurs to describe what they believe is the single most important quality that investors are looking for. Their answer: passion.

For the investors, I similarly ask them to describe what they believe is the single most important attribute that they look for in making their investment decisions, and again, overwhelmingly, it's passion. Some, like Mark Suster, state it immediately. "The goal is to invest in passionate entrepreneurs. That's it, end of story. Passion," he often says, unapologetically.

Other investors will describe it in a more offhand manner—for example, an investor once told me, "I want someone who, at four o'clock in the morning, would not be able to go to bed because they are so excited."

Another shared, "This gal, she would light up when she talked about her business. She was so interested in anything that I would say. She just had to make it work, and the intensity of her passion was just obvious."

Still others try to provide more of a philosophy to back up their assertion, explaining what this passion means and why it is so important to them:

> Ninety percent of success in anything comes from just giving a shit. The older I get, the more amazed I am at how many entrepreneurs just really don't. Ten percent is skill and luck, but just caring enough, having passion about something, means that they will do their best. If they have passion, they will not fail one way or the other, and that matters more than you can imagine.

In my research, I've tested the perceived passion of an entrepreneur, and investors are right—it does matter. It is actually one of the most significant factors in determining who receives start-up funding. I've found that entrepreneurs presenting in pitch competitions who are rated high on passion by investors are 7.4 times more likely to receive funding than those who are rated low on passion. In fact, perceptions of passion compensated for poor performance and weak objective data on the venture—things like profitability, product performance, and market size.

It's no wonder that entrepreneurs feel the need to show passion when they are presenting their ventures to investors—and they often ask me how they can do it. Other scholars have tried to pinpoint what passion is, as well. For example, Melissa Cardon, a professor at Pace University, along with several colleagues who also study entrepreneurial passion, defines it as "an entrepreneur's intense positive feelings that [are] the result of their engagement in entrepreneurial activities."

The influence of such passion is that it presumably impacts an investor's own levels of passion—whereby they experience a change in their own internal emotions. I've heard this echoed by investors as well, who say things like "He was so passionate about it that it made me passionate about it. I could feel myself getting excited in the same way he was."

So to gain an edge, at least in the start-up world, the trick is to be self-aware and pinpoint how you can demonstrate your passion in a more focused, self-enhancing manner, right? Well, not exactly.

First off, what I've discovered is that in the minds of investors, they don't actually know what they're referring to when they say they want a passionate entrepreneur. That is, investors don't agree on what passion is; different investors have different definitions of what it means. Some investors think it's about an entrepreneur demonstrating passion for the vision of the company—that you believe in what you're working on. Others think it's about demonstrating commitment—having the type of passion that can sustain you through the rough cycles. Some investors see these as being linked, while others argue that it's two entirely different things. So as an entrepreneur, you might be trying to enhance in the very ways that would turn one investor on and turn another very much off.

But it's not just differences between investors—in which one investor thinks passion means X, while another thinks passion means Y. Often, when I pushed individual investors, even gently, to define passion, they couldn't. To illustrate: One day an investor told me that he doesn't invest in anyone who doesn't have passion. But then, not more than five minutes later, when I asked him to tell me about an entrepreneur whom he decided *not* to invest in, even though all the objective business data was telling him that it was a good investment, he told me, "Well, there was this one guy who looked like he had had waaaay too much coffee. He was so passionate, and I couldn't invest in him." People might think they want one thing, but that can change at any time.

Not only do people not know what they are looking for in others, they're not likely to notice even if you feel that you are being particularly compelling in demonstrating your passion—or charisma, as it were. This type of "spotlight effect" occurs everywhere. As humans, we all tend to forget that although we are at the center of our own world, we are not at the center of everyone else's. We drastically overestimate the effect we have on others.

We need to train ourselves to redirect that spotlight and get people emotionally invested in people other than themselves. Guiding entails being purposeful in helping others frame the attributions that they make about us.

• • •

Gary Vaynerchuk, the mastermind behind Wine Library and Vayner-Media, once told me, "There is not a single person's opinion that bothers me. I have no expectations of anyone." I called bullshit (his term, not mine) on this pretty quickly, pointing out how much of the success of his companies depends on his public persona and how he is able to deftly interrelate his sense of self with other people's perceptions of him. He is unrepentantly who he is while simultaneously harmonizing with what people think of him. He replied by retorting, "Nope, I'd literally walk away from VaynerMedia and start all over. I think that would be fine and I would make something else incredible. I think that would be fun." Which proved my point exactly.

Gary, as opposed to me, was not a good student in high school. I don't say this with any sort of grandiosity (he does, after all, have a net worth of over $160 million, whereas my net worth is closer to . . . well, never mind). And I only know that he wasn't a good student because we both attended the same high school—a public high school in middle-of-nowhere New Jersey. Rather than endeavoring to earn gold stars, Gary occupied his free time with a small side business selling and trading baseball cards. He started out by going to baseball card shows at a local mall, where he would pay a table fee of $100 to $150, and then try to make a profit selling the cards. When he wasn't selling cards, he was helping out at his dad's wine and liquor store, where he would help crush ice, stock shelves, and manage inventory.

Gary told me once that if he was to have just been himself, he would have spent his early twenties watching sports and looking at baseball cards. But he cultivated a strong sense of self-awareness very early on, and despite his protestations otherwise, he found a way to guide in a manner that allowed him to reconcile who he was with his external responsibilities—namely, the expectation that he join the family business. He said, "I realized that wine is no different than baseball cards. We had the *Beckett Monthly* and every month it came out with what cards were going up and what cards were going down. And with wine we had the *Wine Spectator* that rates wines and dictates what every retailer tries to buy and sell. It's basically the same thing. I would joke about it."

Upon graduating from college, Gary joined the wine and liquor store full-time and started applying some of the techniques that he had learned from selling baseball cards to help his dad make larger profits. He reminisces, "Instead of 'Hey, what about this baseball card?' now it was 'Hey, what about this wine promotion?' or 'What about carrying this type of wine?'" Inexhaustible, he would come up with fifteen or twenty such ideas every day.

Gary, along with his best friend, Brandon, who eventually joined the store as well, continued to formulate ideas for how they could drive more revenue to the store by turning it into a major wine store. Quite quickly, he began to face barriers and realized that he was at a disadvantage relative to others in the industry—he was considered too young and too inexperienced to be a wine connoisseur. His family didn't own a vineyard, just a discount wine and liquor store. He was perceived to be completely unconventional in his thinking, and others in the industry resented that he didn't respect the sanctity of the wine business.

Gary and Brandon knew that to be seen as a major wine store in the eyes of customers, they would need to keep up with trends first and foremost—just as they had kept up with athletes and trends in selling baseball cards. They began to connect with premier wine-producing areas, beginning with a few big but lesser known importers from both Australia and Spain. Over time, this garnered them a huge selection of some of the best wines from emerging regions that would later become regarded as prestigious collectible wines. This then gave them access to more traditional collectibles, such as Insignia, Dominus, Caymus, wines that you previously could get only if you knew the owner or had your name on a special list.

Gary began to connect and engage with customers, and realized that while the wine world was very elitist, he saw wine as something that should be widely accessible. Just as he was seen as unconventional, so too were many consumers. In this way, his unconventional background helped him tap into a market of unconventional customers.

Gary began to build a customer list and openly offer quality wines to all, providing everyone with the opportunity to access high-end collectibles, Spanish and Australian imports, and other new and upcoming wine regions. He started a fax service to fax people offers in the middle of the night. Before leaving his store at nine p.m., he would set up a fax to go out at three a.m. advertising all the high-end collectibles that they had. The idea was that in the morning, people would come into the office and find wine offers on their fax machines. It was Gary's way of getting out large amounts of information to customers quickly with just the push of a button.

As business improved, their fax service evolved into an email service. Gary started emailing thank-you notes to each of his customers, and then he started sending attachments of short videos of him personally saying thank you.

These videos led to other videos, in which he continued to try to make wine accessible to everyone by posting short instructional clips on wine and wine tasting. Gary's friendly and approachable demeanor resonated with his viewers, and soon he found that he had a huge audience—which led to a video blog on YouTube called *Wine Library TV* and an eventual rebranding of their liquor and wine store into Wine Library, a platform that offered online sales and a wine-delivery service, currently bringing in more than $60 million in annual sales. Gary now also owns VaynerMedia, a social media–focused digital agency, where he helps companies create an accessible persona and brand just as he did for Wine Library; as well as VaynerSports, a full-service sports agency; a shoe line with K-Swiss; and his own YouTube show called *The #AskGaryVee Show*.

Those who know Gary describe him as straightforward, real, and raw. He is immensely self-aware. Gary doesn't often mention that his road to success was paved with lots of biased perceptions from others, especially from those who were in the wine industry early on. He was truly an unconventional player in the wine world because of his lack of experience, as well as his youth and background.

But what gave him his edge was being unapologetic about who he is, while simultaneously being attuned to the perceptions of others so that he could align his strengths with the opportunities he saw in his external surroundings to connect and engage with customers. He relied on his strengths—a casual, approachable demeanor—to create associations with customers and suppliers. He was able to guide wine consumers in a way that others could not. He delighted them with his no-nonsense, brash perspective on wine, and enriched them with a new type of experience with wine.

• • •

Hearing Gary's story, it seems simple. But Gary did not fit in. He was not part of the wine elite. Often when we're confronted with situations like Gary's—feeling out of place or unqualified—we try to fake it till we make it.

Remember that *we all have something*. Perceptions and attributions are being made about all of us—and getting into a contest about who has more privilege is not likely to lead to your own long-term success. In the long-term, on a macro level, posturing and faking it provides just temporary value. It doesn't endure, and what ends up being more long-standing is a belief that inevitably holds people back—an enduring feeling of uncertainty and self-doubt. The fear that you will be stereotyped will be more pervasive than any amount of "elite brass" that you can channel, and you will start to anticipate situations in which you may not be as valued as you should be, in turn leading to more self-doubt.

This was what I experienced in all those engineering classes years ago, as one of four females majoring in electrical engineering, where none of us exactly fit the masculine persona—yet we all tried to act that part.

Scholars have found this exact type of posturing in women in mathematics and women and minorities in the workplace—finding that while it does provide some temporary respite, it nonetheless has negative effects on perceptions of performance in the long term.

. . .

And thus, it was quite by accident that I discovered my elite brass equivalent (or as a good friend calls it, carrying herself with the confidence of a "mediocre white male"). That is to say, my personal solution to how I should be framing the conversation when I found myself in those situations in which the culture, the norms, and the environment were dictated by the "elite"—or any fill-in-the-blank type of person (my recent favorite version of the instruction is to "act like Oprah": channel what you think Oprah would do) that I, quite simply, am not.

That was certainly true for me, as I discovered early in my career. Recognizing that guiding myself by acting like someone I wasn't (whether a white man or Oprah) had tended to get me into trouble, I had just given up. I found that overwhelmingly, when I acted like a man—or how I thought a man would stereotypically act—I got push-back. People saw me as aggressive, and I had nothing to show for it.

I had just started a new job, and a trusted mentor had told me that in my new role, it was critical for me to be good at networking and making connections with those in power. He advised me to reach out to people, be assertive, and ask them to coffee. I followed his advice and I did manage to make a few connections and set up a few coffee meetings.

After a few of these encounters, however, I noticed that it was feeling superficial—like I wasn't really getting to know these people. They would offer me the same sort of surface-level advice, and I seemed to be having the same conversations over and over: they were glad to have me, the company provides wonderful opportunities to those who work hard and seek out stretch assignments, and I should get to know lots of people. I didn't really feel like I was making any meaningful connections with any of these people.

And yet, all around me, I'd hear my colleagues saying things like such and such VP "took me to this awesome sushi place and totally hooked me up with the tech team," and such and such managing director "invited me to join him at the sales awards meeting," and even things like "Oh, I'm so wasted. I was doing shots last night with such and such senior head until three a.m."

I was clearly not as proficient in my networking. Again, I received advice along the lines of: "You need to do that—invite people to lunch, invite them out for drinks, not just normal coffee meetings." But in the back of my mind, I remember thinking, "Me? As a young Asian female? I should be inviting my senior male colleagues out for drinks?" There was no way that was going to happen. I knew intuitively that I was not going to be able to pull that one off.

But a few weeks later, I discovered that I too had the ability to make connections with senior leaders in my organization—authentic connections, even more so than I had imagined. I was scheduled to give a presentation at an industry conference and was taking an early flight to get there. It wasn't until we landed and I got off the plane that I saw that the senior VP of the division I belonged to was on the same flight.

I went over and said hello, and asked him if he had flown in for the same conference and was planning to attend, or if he was in town for other business. He indicated that he was attending the same confer-ence and then asked me, "How are you getting to the conference cen-ter?" I told him that I was going to catch a cab, to which he replied, "Oh, I have a driver coming to pick me up." (Of course he did. I too was having a driver come to pick me up . . . only my driver works for a cab company, and his private driver works for him.)

But then he offered, "Do you want to catch a ride with me?"

Over the course of the forty-five-minute drive, we chatted and he got to know me, on neutral turf where I felt confident and comfortable. Not in a restaurant or bar, where I would feel the need to make that time worth his while; where I would feel the need to impress him, or be interesting or insightful so I wouldn't feel bad about asking him to drinks. Or where I felt like I had to have some agenda (which would be clear to him). Here, I could just be myself.

There was no time pressure, no meeting for him to rush off to. We were captive for forty-five minutes and just enjoyed the time. Our con-versation progressed naturally, like conversations are meant to when you're merely trying to get to know someone with no alternate agenda. I asked him for advice on things that came up organically; I was witty and let my natural sense of humor show. And he saw that I was a smart, insightful person. He got to know my personality.

At the conference, even though he was running between meet-ings, he made the time to catch the last ten minutes of my presentation and then came up to me to tell me how well he thought it went. He told me that I was a natural presenter. A few weeks later, he invited me to give a presentation to his internal team. To this day, he remains one of my most trusted and closest mentors.

It is stories like this one and the one with Gary of Wine Library and VaynerMedia that I hope you remember when thinking about guiding others' views of you. Gary didn't pretend to be a snooty, typical wine elitist, and I didn't try to be one of the bros doing sake bombs. We can't try to cater to what we think others want, because we have no idea how to do that, or what they want, and they don't know either. Instead, we have to be opportunistic and savvy in seizing chances to demonstrate who we really are, and be unapologetic and confident.

Guiding others does not have to be arduous or painful, nor does it have to be an act that takes you out of your own comfort zone. It can be a simple by-product and an organic extension of your surroundings. Let things work for you, especially in guiding perceptions about you.

PRINCIPLE 11

Guide others to what is within you by recognizing what is around you.

CHAPTER 12

You Need at Least Two Points to Create a Trajectory

You have the power to say, "This is not how the story is going to end."

—Cindy Eckert

IT'S NOT JUST WHO YOU ARE AS AN INDIVIDUAL THAT OTHERS will be judging. People will also be judging your path—the trajectory of where you have been, and where they think you are going.

The trajectory of an academic is often expected to follow an apprenticeship model. Advisors take students under their wing, teach them their craft, and then release them into a world of academia and boundless economic opportunity.

I was fortunate in landing my first academic placement after that propitious dinner with Raffi and Mac, if you'll recall. But the part of the story that I left out is what led up to the invitation to visit with them in the first place.

Before you're even at the stage of being invited to visit the school, there is a four-to-six-month lead-up—a period when you must substantiate that you are a well-trained apprentice. In my field, organizational and behavioral science, when you're in the last year of your doctoral program, you go "on the market" and start looking for either a postdoc position or an academic position at a college or university.

There is a ton of strategizing and advance preparation that goes into this process. Months before, students are advised to start putting together their packet of materials, which are eventually sent to all the colleges and universities to which you'll be applying. This packet includes a résumé, multiple writing samples, a research statement that outlines the importance of your scholarship, a teaching statement that outlines your pedagogical philosophy, and multiple letters of recommendation.

Prior to sending out formal applications and packets, students also attend our field-wide academic conference, the Academy of Management conference, attended by more than ten thousand people each year. At this conference, students attend networking events, start to set up some initial interviews with some of the schools that they are interested in, and try to talk to as many people as they can. Those who are on the market are easy to identify—they are the ones in full business suits, while everyone else is dressed much more casually.

In the year that I was on the market, my dear advisor (the master to this humble apprentice) made it a point to give me one particular piece of advice: "Be the prom queen."

I remember looking at her and thinking, "Wait, that's the only advice you're going to give me?" In the four years I had spent working with her, I had never left a meeting without hordes of advice about my research, what improvements I should be making, what I should be working on, things that I should think about, how to think about my data. Every manuscript I had sent to my advisor would be returned with pages and pages of comments, things crossed out in red, notes and feedback in the margins of each page, scribbles of revisions, and suggestions and items to think about. But for the process I was about to embark on, which would be the culmination of my PhD career, the only thing she had to offer was "Be the prom queen"?

And so I sputtered out, incredulously, "Be the prom queen? What does that mean?" I needed clarification. Her reply: "Everyone wants to date the prom queen." And then she sent me on my way.

• • •

Truth be told, I was far from the actual prom queen in real life. And I certainly was far from the social science equivalent of the prom queen. You see, the main currency that academics have in the field is their publications. Of which I had none. Publish or perish, baby. By the time doctoral students go on the market, they often have multiple publications, or at the very least, one—preferably in a top-tier journal. These are the students who command the most attention from universities; these are the students who land the plum academic jobs.

In lieu of top-tier publications, search committees will sometimes significantly weight the quality of the institution from which you're receiving your PhD, as a signal that you have the academic chops to publish in top-tier publications, even if you haven't yet done so. And there is a clear hierarchy of these research institutions—typically schools like MIT, Stanford, and Yale are considered top-of-the-line, but well-known public research universities like University of Michigan, UT Austin, and University of North Carolina also carry immense influence.

I had neither going for me—neither any publications to my name nor a high-caliber school to back me. My doctorate would be from UC

Irvine, which often does not even make the list of the top fifty research institutions.*

And so I pondered why my advisor felt that I had it in me to be the prom queen. Perhaps it was just that she was like a mother; every mother thinks that their kid is the prettiest in the class and should be the prom queen, right?

My advisor's advice kept plaguing me, even as I started networking and meeting with people at the Academy of Management conference. It was there that I met the prom royalty, so to speak—a handful of men and women in my cohort who had multiple top-tier publications, were being wined and dined by professors at top schools, and had plenty of charisma that captivated everyone around them.

In that instant, in addition to realizing that I, in fact, was *not* the prom queen, I also understood that a number of schools were doing intimate, invitation-only chats with people they knew to be on the market. My attempts at networking with folks at these schools would be, at best, feeble.

When I saw my advisor later that evening, she asked me, "Well, were you the prom queen?" To which I replied, "No, but I did meet the prom queen." She was only slightly amused, and then she went on to explain that it didn't matter that I wasn't coming from the top institution, because I was well trained. My advisor didn't think any of that should stand in the way of a belief that I could fare just as well as, if not

---

* Though I do feel the need to defend my alma mater. Getting my PhD from UC Irvine is something that I will never regret, and will forever be grateful for. It was the best training ground I could have asked for. I wouldn't trade my experiences or my education there for anything. Every person I worked with at UC Irvine had my best interests at heart, and I never thought to think differently. It was truly a nurturing environment. And I think it goes without saying that my advisor is absolutely matchless. May every doctoral student have the opportunity to work with someone as selfless, talented, and dedicated as my advisor was.

better than, others. It didn't matter that I didn't have the most publications (or any at all), because that wasn't the journey I'd had, nor the trajectory that she believed I *would* have.

She had expected me to guide the understanding that while I hadn't had the normal trajectory that we expect to see in a doctoral student—one in which you work hard, make steady progress, and then have a paper or two to show for yourself—I hadn't had the traditional apprenticeship trajectory either. Mine wasn't the model of a *steady, upward trajectory* of someone who is taken on as the student of someone famous, groomed to produce a certain type of work, and then able to show the fruits of that labor.

"But that's what makes you uncommon," she said. "That's what makes you special. That's what makes you the prom queen—someone who generates the interest, demand, and attention of everyone, based on the aura of something special. That you're on an uncommon, *special* trajectory. Guide people to *that,* you dummy." (She didn't actually say that last part.)

Don't let them make assumptions. Don't let them decide where "your story is going to end", as Cindy Eckert says. Give them the data points so that they can draw the trend line that *you* want them to see. Tell them, rather than allowing them to guess, about your future potential. Indeed, embrace and exert power over your life narrative. Tell them that you have so much farther to go.

My journey, my trajectory, was one in which I was not told what to do, but was instead given support and encouragement to explore my own research passions. Where others had been *given* a passion project, I had discovered mine by having to go out there myself to struggle and figure out a phenomenon. In turn, I had answered an unanswered, previously unsolvable question: the role of gut feel in entrepreneurial investment decisions—something that very much ran counter to traditional economic theory and entrepreneurial finance, which no one else had dared study. And as a result, I had produced one of the most novel and interesting dissertation topics out there.

This trajectory wasn't the shiniest or prettiest—but it did offer something special and unique. No one else had had the trajectory that I'd had, nor the story and the resulting research that I had to offer.

. . .

You already know how this story ends—how I found myself at a steak dinner in Philadelphia, and ultimately landed my first academic position. What I haven't said yet is that I ended up sitting down the hall from one of those famous professors, who I remember was wining and dining and wooing others. Years later, he told me in passing that I was hired because I was seen as an "unfinished work"—someone with a fresh, new, and distinctive way of looking at the literature, with an amazing trajectory and tons of upside potential. It was basically the same thing that my advisor had said.

Being the prom queen, I discovered, truly is about the aura of something special. It's about mapping and explaining where you have come from and where you are going, in a way that guides others to understand your value. Too often, we try to follow the trajectory that others have taken, using it as a road map for success and trying to contort our own experiences into the standard trajectory. But had I attempted to sell myself with the tried-and-true academic trajectory— the type that others embodied—it would have gone horribly wrong.

. . .

What is it about trajectories? Why are they important? First, being able to clearly communicate your trajectory allows you to guide people in such a way that they can comprehend who you are in a coherent and meaningful way. Some may call it a personal narrative, but it's more than that. A narrative provides an anecdote, a moral, a quick lesson, like what you'd get from one of Aesop's fables. A trajectory, on the other hand, paints a richer picture of where you are and where you have come from—who you are as a person and what others can expect of you. This trajectory, importantly, lets *you* dictate what is meaningful for them to know. *You* get to package factual information about both your tangibles and your intangibles—you get to be the one to construct it. They don't. That is important. There will always be people trying to project a description onto you, trying to tell you who they think you are based on signals that they pick up on, cues that they notice—and biases that they draw from. When you take control of the trajectory that you've experienced, it's the equivalent of taking over the steering wheel and constructing the sequence for them before they have a chance to do so. You anchor them at a point that *you* dictate, rather than letting them construct a view of you that you might then need to spend all your energy getting them to think differently about and trying to prove yourself otherwise.

This is what I eventually did with job search committees. Rather than letting them write me off because I didn't have any publications, I took the steering wheel and communicated how my trajectory had led me to a novel, never-before-seen research contribution. And so senior faculty members went beyond their initial signals and cues. They overcame their uncertainty and risk avoidance that otherwise would have disqualified a candidate from a lower-tier university, to understand how I could be that diamond in the rough.

In this way, a clear and fitting trajectory also allows you to help others understand your value and how you will enrich. What do you want people to know about your trajectory—where you have been and where you are going? What is it about your trajectory that helps people understand your potential and your ability to enrich?

You can immediately help them do their sense-making around understanding how who you are and where you've been will bring potential value. You won't have to explicitly elaborate complex reasoning behind how you're going to get from point X to point Y, because your story allows them to make that leap on their own. Your trajectory provides the handholds and the logic that allow them to do it on their own, which is not only more powerful but also more memorable.

Finally, a proper trajectory helps generate interest and commitment. You've directed others to your upside potential and you've primed them on what your future trajectory might be. Effectively communicating your trajectory allows others to connect what you are saying to a broader context. Make no mistake, your depiction and your trajectory are yours—so it will still appear original and distinctive to others—but just by painting a picture of where you have been and where you are now, you allow people to embed what you are saying within broader contexts that are interesting to them.

• • •

So how do you grasp and recognize your trajectory—the trajectory that will give you your edge? It's about recognizing the path you have taken thus far, and the path you intend to take going forward. Many different trajectories exist—like the steady, *upward trajectory* that we discussed, or the *distance-traveled trajectory* or *second-chances trajectory*, as we'll soon see, but these are just a few. Yours may be some variation of these or something entirely different. Daniel Bertaux and Martin Kohli, sociologists who examine the use of life stories and autobiographical narratives, find that there is no comprehensive set of archetypes to describe one's trajectory—but instead, there are two main trends. The first focuses on meaning and patterns, and the other focuses on what shaped these patterns within the social milieu. In other words, the logic *and* the larger paradigm. Your trajectory has to provide an account of the details that really matter, but if you don't know how each detail fits into the overall story of what really matters, you don't really understand it and you can't effectively communicate it. But communicating your trajectory isn't just about storytelling and isn't just about being cute. To pinpoint your trajectory, you must understand and appreciate the underlying disadvantages, challenges, and obstacles that you face and have faced and the ongoing path that you see yourself on.

My friend Beatriz's path is about how far she has traveled, from bookkeeper to Louis Vuitton—quite effortlessly, it seems. When I met Beatriz on the first day of our MBA program, I was immediately struck by how unbelievably poised she was, dressed in a style that was uniquely hers—professional and practiced, yet effortless and chic. It was only months later that I learned about how she had grown up in an extremely small rural town in Spain, where her childhood was spent helping her family tend farmland. Until the day she left, she had never ventured more than about thirty-five miles outside her town, let alone left the country.

She had achieved quite a lot by the time she left Spain, by her town's standards, having gotten some basic bookkeeping training and even landing a job as a receptionist at one of the larger offices in the next town. But one day, she decided that she was going to move to Germany, a country she had always dreamed of seeing. To her and her friends, it was a place that could provide something bigger, something greater than what they were destined for at home, even greater than anything Spain could provide.

So she saved up, took a chance, and moved to Munich. She started interviewing for whatever jobs she could—in German. The first few interviews were, predictably, quite disastrous (and as she recounts it, quite humorous), as she spoke no German at all, and even if her interviewers spoke Spanish they didn't let on. But she owned it, and kept at it, acknowledging her language deficiency. She noticed that when she openly told her interviewers that she was from Spain and that her German was still evolving, they would do most of the talking—they even seemed to enjoy doing so. As Beatriz recounts, "I started noticing that some of the questions were the same. And I would listen to them talk about their companies and almost answer the question themselves."

She would listen. And then she started memorizing certain phrases, not knowing what those phrases even meant. She found that almost instinctually, at the next interview, she'd repeat some of those phrases she picked up here and there—just to keep up with the conversation. "Lots of times, I didn't even know what it was that I was saying. I was just stringing together words and sentences—things that I had heard and that sounded good," she told me.

People found it charming. She was amazed. She would infuse her own interpretation of things that she only barely understood, and then be complimented for taking a risk. She recalls, "They said that I was distinctive. One person even told me that they thought I would go very far in life."

She started to realize that people took to her. More specifically, they took to the *distance-traveled* trajectory. When they would ask her to tell them about herself, she would guide them through her trajectory: coming from a small town in Spain, but having the guts and fortitude and gumption to not only operate in a foreign language, but to do so with her own flavor of poise and sophistication.

And then one day, she had an interview at a company that she had never heard of: Goldman Sachs. They were looking for a receptionist in their private wealth management area. The minute she set foot into the company, she knew that what they wanted was a receptionist who was professional and practiced, yet effortless and chic. She guided them through her trajectory, stringing together phrases that sounded good, even while not speaking German fluently. They loved that she could improvise and charm while still not having command of the language—and in fact, they saw that as a huge asset, especially with their client base, many of whom were also not native German speakers. She got the job.

She was a spectacular receptionist. Within a year, they promoted her to analyst—the first time they had ever promoted a receptionist to a frontline role. Her manager had made the case that she had made great progress, and that she continued to show guts and gumption, poise and sophistication time and time again—her trajectory. And then shortly after, she was promoted to sales associate in private wealth management. They gave her the opportunity to take stretch assignments in Frankfurt, New York, Miami, and Switzerland.

She soon left Goldman Sachs to pursue her MBA, which is when I met her. She wanted to make a switch into luxury goods—which proved to be difficult, though the industry requires the very qualities that she had been building throughout her entire trajectory. Even as we faced our impending graduation date, she still had no job. Yet while others who also had no offers were nervously scrambling, she just reminded herself that what she was experiencing was merely what had been foreshadowed in the past, in the early days of her trajectory. Instead of not speaking German, this time she didn't "speak" luxury goods.

Three months later, she received an offer from LVMH (Louis Vuitton) as their manager for women's leather goods in Paris at Maison Champs-Élysées. She started out on the sales floor managing sales associates, but it surprised no one when she became store director for Louis Vuitton in Monaco, responsible for the store's revenue and profitability targets, local marketing, operations, HR, and team management, and later also taking on responsibility for Louis Vuitton in Milan, managing private client relations and client events.

. . .

Beatriz's trajectory helped her communicate an important account of who she is: gutsy, risk-taking, sophisticated, and poised under any circumstance. Yes, she started off from humble beginnings. Yes, she probably felt at times like she had to work twice as hard as everyone else. But as she noted to me on multiple occasions, all of that was irrelevant. People don't even notice (or care about) effort. At first, they judged Beatriz the same as everyone else—as if everyone began at the same start line. It was how she communicated and positioned her trajectory that changed that. It was her trajectory that enamored them, allowing them to see that she had actually come very far on very few resources (and in spite of lots of hurdles), and she was able to deliver her brand of sophistication—the very characteristic they valued and appreciated—precisely because of the path she had taken.

For others, it's not about coming from humble beginnings and showing the distance they have traveled. The world can be cruel at times, and someone like Dave Dahl, whose trajectory is based on what someone can do with a second chance in life, can tell you that it was the story he was able to tell because of this second chance that gave him his edge.

Dave had spent fifteen years in and out of prison for drug abuse, robbery, and assault. He found himself labeled as an ex-con and a failure. But his identity wasn't always tied so tightly to such labels. Dave conveys the days from his childhood when he found that he had a gift for making bread. And that led to him deciding that he would try to turn this gift into part of his salvation: he would make breads that were nutritious, natural, and filled with seeds, nuts, and grains,* and slowly try to build himself back up. The only problem? He saw the way

* Perfect for someone on the Paleo diet, were it not for the bread part. . .

people reacted to his ponytail, gravelly voice, and overall demeanor, and knew that starting a bread company was going to be a tough road. The distance-traveled trajectory was never going to work for him. But he could do something else—he could own his failures and present his own trajectory. He started his company, calling it Dave's Killer Bread, with the description of the company mirroring the trajectory of his life:

> At Dave's Killer Bread, we have witnessed the power of Second Chance Employment: hiring those who have a criminal background, and are ready to change their lives for the better. It gives people a second chance not only to make a living, but make a life.
>
> Without employment opportunities, those with criminal backgrounds often resort to the only life they know—a life of crime. We want to change that.

Dave guided not only investors but also retailers and customers to see why his trajectory warranted a second chance. Turn it into your advantage and make it about guts. Remember that 75 percent of super-high achievers come from troubled families—the types of families who have found success from a second chance.

This can be harnessed to guide. Describe your failure, your trajectory, without bitterness: "It has been an incredible journey." "I learned a ton." It presents every failure as temporary—a way station to success.

. . .

There are many trajectories and many ways to depict your own trajectory. We've discussed a few here, but it is nowhere near a comprehensive list. There isn't one path that is "better" than another, because your edge comes from recognizing the corresponding impressions that others will have of you based on the path you have taken and the path you intend to take, and how to manage and guide those impressions.

The way you chronicle your personal trajectory helps you explain who you are in a compelling way, a way that others will understand and be impacted by. People are trying to guess about your future potential based on your past trajectory. Ultimately, there is no wrong or right trajectory. The only mistake you can make is having no trajectory in mind at all. If you don't provide your own chronicle of who you are, one will be given to you. You'll assume whatever description the other party gives you, dictated by *their* biases, perceptions, and attributions. Don't passively let others write your narrative—write *your own* narrative and guide others' view of you. Make sure you have a baseline account of your trajectory, craft your own narrative, and don't shy away from embracing all your past experiences—even the disadvantages, challenges, and obstacles that you've faced—in mapping your story. Your past is not something that you should lament; it should be another asset in how you gain your unique advantage. Let your past make you better, not bitter.

PRINCIPLE 12

It's not where you've *been*; it's where you're *going*. Guide how others see your trajectory.

PART 4

Effort

CHAPTER 13

Reinforcing Your Edge

You are always one decision away from a totally different life.

—Author unknown

WHEN I WAS WORKING IN PHILADELPHIA, I DID A LOT OF WALKING, so I had distances timed down to the minute. The walk from my office to Trader Joe's? Twelve minutes. The nearest coffee shop? Three minutes. My office to the Thirtieth Street train station? Eighteen minutes.

One day a speaker visited us. As he was heading out, he asked how long it would take him to get to the train station if he was going to walk rather than take a taxi. We told him that he should budget thirty minutes to be safe.

"What if I'm a fast walker?" he asked.

Almost in unison, three different people responded. One of my colleagues answered, "Twenty minutes," another colleague answered, "Twenty-three minutes," while I said, obviously, "Eighteen minutes."

Much to the dismay of this speaker, anxious to get on his way, my colleagues and I started debating—the route we took, the shortcuts we used, where there were longer walk signals. Neither of them believed that I could make it in eighteen minutes.

Here's what we discovered. First, yes, it was conceivable that I could make it in eighteen minutes based on the route I took and the specific approach I employed. "Approach" may sound like a funny way to describe my walk from the office to the train station, but that's exactly what it was.

When I first started making that walk, it was my first time living in a big city, and I found myself having to travel quite a bit on the commuter line originating from the Thirtieth Street station. Not knowing my way around, and not having a handle on my schedule yet, I missed my train a number of times because I had budgeted only twenty minutes.

I started exploring shortcuts—taking one street that ran diagonally seemed to save me a bit of time, and going around the Drexel campus rather than cutting through it saved me more time than I expected because I didn't have to dodge all the students milling around.

And perhaps the biggest time-saver was reading the lights and walk signals. This was how I ultimately cut the walk down to eighteen minutes, and I even got down to sixteen minutes one glorious day. Even with the same route and the same average speed, by reading the signals, I was able to make my commute that much more efficient.

I would look ahead to see what signal was showing on the pedestrian crossing. When it showed a stop signal, I would slow down and conserve my energy. When I saw that there were ten seconds left on the walk signal, I would speed up, walk briskly, and make damn sure that I made that crosswalk.

Explaining all this to my colleagues made me realize that having your hard work *work* for you is not unlike this approach of mine.

Where you put in your effort makes a difference: identifying where you want to take the diagonal streets rather than the parallel streets, where you want to go around rather than pass through (even when passing through appears simpler at first glance), when to conserve and ease up on your pace, and when to dig in and make a surge.

• • •

effort /ˈefərt/
a vigorous or determined attempt

Throughout this book, I've been vague concerning my real views on effort and hard work. I've said that hard work is critical. And I stand by that. I've also alluded to my belief that hard work doesn't speak for itself—we need hard work, *plus.*

I would never say that telling someone to work hard and put in effort is bad advice. But it just seems so obvious and basic. It doesn't seem very helpful, particularly when it's presented as the panacea for getting a job or receiving some accolade or reward. And yet, I keep hearing people giving this advice and explaining that hard work was the key to their own achievements. "Just keep working hard. Just keep chasing your dreams. The rewards will follow."

We all know there's actually a multitude of reasons why someone gets the desired outcome. Luck is one. Systemic privilege is another. And an edge is yet another. Enrich, Delight, Guide, and Effort—these are the components to creating your own edge.

It is my hope that reading this book has helped you see how you can create your own edge so that your hard work works harder for you—in spite of any apparent privilege, disadvantage, or bias that is out there and that you might experience.

When you are able to demonstrate how you enrich and provide value; when you open doors for yourself by delighting others; when you can guide the perceptions that others have of you—that's when your hard work and effort work harder for you. There are instances in which you may *seemingly* be at a disadvantage according to conventional wisdom and based on things like gender, race, ethnicity, age, wealth, and class—but you can turn things around to create some sort of gain or reward for yourself regardless of any apparent advantage or privilege.

Effort should reinforce the edge that you create for yourself. That means putting your effort into the things that allow you to enrich, delight, and guide—and it necessitates relinquishing the bitterness and resentment that so many of us hold on to because of the obstacles, drawbacks, disadvantages, and adversity we've experienced. We've heard many people's stories of and journeys through disadvantage, underestimation, and bias. They are incredible examples of creating an edge against all odds. I've also touched on some of my own, and in my journey from adversity to advantage, I've realized that creating an edge is never a once-and-for-all exercise. Mine, and yours, will continue to require a revisiting of all the nuances that provide us with our unique ability to enrich, delight, guide, and put forth effort.

• • •

When I said that being an engineer was my first career, I wasn't being completely truthful. Sure, most people would consider engineering to be my first career, but only because I've rarely shared what, in my heart, I consider my first career.

It was nearly twenty years ago, and I had just finished a master's degree in engineering, knowing I should probably do something with the degree that I had worked so hard for. In addition to working toward the degree, I'd had to work multiple jobs at the same time—twenty hours a week building servers at IBM, as well as working at the university housing office and the university library. And yet, as I graduated, I found myself hesitant to accept that full-time job that I was offered at IBM, which offered me more money than I had ever thought possible.

As you know by now, I had always felt a pull toward math. So imagine the horror of my mother—who was at this point a single mother trying to raise two children—when I told her I wanted to try out teaching math. I had a degree in engineering, not in education, she said. I had not done a day of teaching in my life—not as a student teacher, not even as a peer tutor, she said. I had no credentials, she said. She was correct on all counts.

And yet, as a testament to how strong and independent a woman she is, she supported me as I started sending out emails to every single school district on the Eastern Seaboard. I got a single positive response, from a public high school in Maryland, which had unexpectedly just had a teacher quit. They were in a bind and wanted to know if I would be willing to teach a course called Related Math. I soon understood this to be a euphemism for "remedial math"—a course designed for ninth and tenth graders who were earmarked as being in the danger zone because of their lack of basic math skills. And would I be able to start in two days?

I said yes. Two days later, I was a teacher at the school. Though it was technically part of a larger school district that was considered fairly well-to-do, the students in this particular school were anything but. The area that this school served was unique in that it had a huge influx of immigrants—who came because of the school district so that they could try to provide a great education for their children, but could only afford to live in this particular area of the district. In my classes, I had students from Panama, Gabon, Cambodia, Vietnam, Thailand, Argentina, Liberia, Philippines, Nicaragua, Nigeria, and numerous other countries. Many of the families came seeking political asylum. The majority of the students were on the government free- or reduced-lunch program.

There is no big story here—I was not Michelle Pfeiffer in *Dangerous Minds*, I was not Hilary Swank in *Freedom Writers*, I was not Robin Williams in *Dead Poets Society*—except that this is where this book began for me. Teaching those children made me burn to understand why some have an edge, and how we can compensate when we don't. Because a piece of my heart was devoted to these kids (and always will be, as I realize between tears; never do I think of them without tears coming to my eyes), and there was nothing more that I wanted during that time in my life than for these kids to find *their* edge.

And yet, I abandoned them. That's the ugly truth. After four months of teaching high school math, I resigned.

One of my students sent me this note shortly after:

hi miss huang just took the time to read ur leter and it is very touching, and very sad dat I wont have u as a teacher anymore boi o boi!

i want to give u props cause as I told u I use to get E's and D's in math but not no more u thought me that math is easy and really funn.

well i will miss u and hope u change ur mind about moving cause it realli sux da ur moving and all.

man its sux dat the last day we get to see u was on the final exams!

wellz fare well to u

peace and love,
jimmy

I loved my kids. But I was frustrated with what I was experiencing and with what my students were experiencing—we were promised that hard work would deliver rewards, but the reality proved otherwise. I had become jaded. I didn't yet understand the power of creating an edge to protect, buffer, and even inoculate against frustration.

I didn't yet know how to help them overcome their challenges, or even believe at that point that they *could*. As a twenty-two-year-old, I wasn't ready yet. Perhaps it was because I wasn't emotionally strong enough, and I selfishly felt the pressure to do something that others would consider more prestigious. It still tears me up thinking that I abandoned them. And that I probably left more than a few of them feeling bitter.

• • •

And then this past year, I had a student in my leadership class at Harvard Business School named Rishabh, who reminded me a lot of a student I'd had in my Related Math class.

Rishabh didn't know about my prior high school teaching experience, nor about the bitterness that I had been carrying around for years—again, I rarely talk openly about either of these things—but he opened up for some reason and told me about how he had grown up in poverty, and how difficult school had been for him. He told me about the nights when his family would go out to a restaurant and share one meal for the entire family. And he admitted that he knew others consistently had low expectations of him. Because of this, always ingrained in the back of his mind was this feeling that it wasn't fair. It made him angry, and this anger would come out at times, even when he didn't realize it. "This bitterness, it colored the way I saw things," he said.

But then he said: "At some point, I let it go. I just decided to let that feeling and that bitterness go. And it was freeing. And it changed everything." And he saw the impact it had on his life, especially when he compared himself with his parents, who still held on to that bitterness; he didn't know if they'd ever be able to let go. Wistful, he added, "It impacts them. It impacts the way that they've been able to live. And that pains me."

. . .

I still think often of Jimmy, and of all of them: Somrit, Tiffaney, Queenstar, Joseph (JJ), Francisco (Franky), Lincoln, Carlos, and many others. I wonder where they are, and with a sense of regret in my heart, I hope with my entire being that they are doing well and that they are happy in life.

What I've finally realized, decades after leaving that high school classroom, is that effort is a double-edged sword. It's necessary; it is the foundation of your edge. But focusing solely on effort to the exclusion of enriching, delighting, and guiding will make you bitter. It will frustrate you to work so hard and not reap proportional results. It will blind you to everything but bias and disadvantage, and it will paralyze you.

And so I end this with where it began for me. The final thought that I want to leave you with is that the optimal conditions for creating an edge are those in which bitterness and regret do not restrain you; they embolden you. Even if you are perfect, the world isn't. Acknowledge and accept this, and you have already begun to create your edge. The secret is to know that the deck is stacked, and that life's not fair. But you put in hard work *plus*, regardless. Don't let success define you, but don't let failure define you either. Play the long game, not the short one.

There will be drawbacks. There will be disappointments. You *will* see the good, the bad, and the ugly. We will all get screwed over.

There will also be haters. The more you do, the more successful you become, the more people will come out of the woodwork to capitalize on it. The more successful you become, the more some people will be biased against you, and the more some will be rooting for you to fail. The more impact, the more influence, the more of an edge you have, the more critics there will be, and the more some will try to bring you down.

We can either let it fester or we can leverage it to make us better.

• • •

A few years ago, I won an award for being one of the top forty professors under the age of forty, and I was asked, "What would you be if you weren't a business school professor?" Without skipping a beat, I nonchalantly said, "I would start a school for underprivileged kids. Maybe I'll still do that someday."

Maybe I will. Maybe someday, I'll return to the high school classroom and teach students like Jimmy and Somrit and Franky again. In the meantime, I see aspects of each of these former students of mine in each of my new students: toughness, strength, and confidence. In Rishabh. In Divinity, who said to me, "It ain't what they call you, it's what you answer to," recounting advice from her grandmother, who was a Mississippi sharecropper's daughter with a fourth-grade education but one of the wisest people she knows. Her sage advice guides the way many of us should show up in the world. And I see it in Cerelina, who I recently took out for a celebratory dinner after she received her GED. She plans to go back to school to study criminal justice. She brought her now two-year-old daughter with her to dinner—her daughter whose middle name is *Rhodes*.

Effort reinforces your edge. It is the mental toughness that underlies all of this, and that toughness provides an inoculation against the disappointments that we all will inevitably face because we remain at the mercy of the perceptions of others. It reminds us that at the end of the day, it's not what others think; it's what you think. You have to know how you enrich. You have to delight yourself and others. And you have to trust in yourself as your guide.

Enrich. Delight. Guide. Effort. Turn adversity into an advantage— turn adversity into *your* edge.

PRINCIPLE 13

Turn adversity into your edge.

EDGE PRINCIPLES

PRINCIPLE 1 • Hard work should speak for itself. (But it doesn't.)

PRINCIPLE 2 • It's not about giving it your all. Your basic goods help you get it all.

PRINCIPLE 3 • To use your basic goods in distinct ways, go where others don't.

PRINCIPLE 4 • Embrace constraints. Constraints provide opportunities.

PRINCIPLE 5 • Your powers of discernment come from trusting your intuition and your experiences.

PRINCIPLE 6 • Before people will let you in, they need to be delighted.

PRINCIPLE 7 • Don't overplan. Instead, aim for flexibility and opportunities to delight.

PRINCIPLE 8 • Stay authentic and embrace how delight occurs in situ.

PRINCIPLE 9 • "Being yourself" entails guiding others to all the glorious versions of yourself.

PRINCIPLE 10 • Know how others see you, so you can redirect them to how they *should* see you.

PRINCIPLE 11 • Guide others to what is within you by recognizing what is around you.

PRINCIPLE 12 • It's not where you've *been*; it's where you're *going*. Guide how others see your trajectory.

PRINCIPLE 13 • Turn adversity into your edge.

ACKNOWLEDGMENTS

I feel incredibly lucky that this book became a reality. And it's not lost on me that behind every instance of luck is someone who made it happen—someone who took a chance on me or gave me a lucky break even when they had no reason to do so. I am indebted to those who set me on a path of luck following luck following luck:

To all those who generously shared and entrusted me with your stories. I will be eternally grateful for your vulnerability, wisdom, and perceptiveness. You've given me dimensionality, purpose, and a calling.

To my agent, Faith Hamlin. You were the one who took a closer look and made this possible. Thank you for believing in me from day one.

To everyone on the Portfolio team, especially my editor, Merry Sun. Thank you for being the embodiment of someone who shrugs off obstacles, keeps calm, and carries on. Without you, I'd be in a fortress rather than an amusement park. Thanks also to the ever astute Adrian Zackheim, and the entire team of Tara Gilbride, Will Weisser, Margot Stamas, Jessica Regione, Daniel Lagin, and Meighan Cavanaugh; Kym

Surridge and Katie Hurley for their keen eyes in the production process; Marisol Salaman, Mary Kate Skehan, and Nicole Dewey for publicity and marketing, who together were able to polish rocks into diamonds; Pete Garceau for an edgier cover design than I could have ever imagined and Chris Sergio for believing that I could pull off something that edgy and indulging me in the artistic process; and Eric Nelson, for giving me entrée into this world.

To those who provided suggestions and feedback, from big things to small, from reading excerpts to vetting cover designs to agonizing with me over subtitles. Lizz Jiang and Libby Quinn, I marvel at my good fortune in working with you both, and value your support more than you know. Thanks also to Ana Homayoun, Katie Barron, Greg Autry, Garrett Neiman, Arlan Hamilton, Scott Barry Kaufman, Katy Milkman, Dolly Chugh, Seth Stephens-Davidowitz, Tracy Chou, Tiffany Chou, Yee Ling Chang, Charles Yao and the entire Lavin team, and Kent Smetters, for your encouragement, advice, and guidance during this process.

To my phenomenal community of collaborators and coauthors—each of you has helped me see the world differently, and none of this is my work alone—it is our work.

To my amazing colleagues at Harvard Business School—it is a blessing to work among your brilliant minds and I am so grateful for your encouragement and support—and to those former colleagues at the Wharton School who embraced me and have remained inspirations.

To Jone Pearce, Raffi Amit, Ian MacMillan, Carrie Knerr O'Brien, Georgia Lazana, Fen Kung, and Chi Chang, for having confidence in me, and allowing me to stand on the shoulders of giants.

And to my faithful family and friends—especially Mama and

Baba, for your strength, savvy, and sacrifice; Chrissy, for thankfully imparting on me some of your wit and charm; and Ant, for the real, the imagined, and all the curiosities in between—you are all my steady reminders to keep the main thing the main thing and to devotedly fight for what's worth fighting for.

INTRODUCTION

2 **Byron knew I was working:** Greg Autry and Laura Huang, "Houston, We Have a Market: Privatizing Space Launches Pays Off Big," *Forbes*, October 2, 2013, https://www.forbes.com/sites/forbesleadershipforum /2013/10/02/houston-we-have-a-market-privatizing-space-launches -pays-off-big; Greg Autry and Laura Huang, "An Anal`ysis of the Competitive Advantage of the United States of America in Commercial Human Orbital Spaceflight Markets," *New Space* 2, no. 2 (2014): 83–110, https:// doi.org/10.1089/space.2014.0005.

4 **Truth be told:** Elon Musk, conversation with author, SpaceX headquarters, Hawthorne, California, February 2, 2015.

6 **Over the course of my career:** Alison Wood Brooks, Laura Huang, Sarah Wood Kearney, and Fiona E. Murray, "Investors Prefer Entrepreneurial Ventures Pitched by Attractive Men," *Proceedings of the National Academy of Sciences* 111, no. 12 (2014): 4427–31, https://doi.org/10.1073/pnas .1321202111. See also Matthew Lee and Laura Huang, "Gender Bias, Social Impact Framing, and Evaluation of Entrepreneurial Ventures," *Organization Science* 29, no. 1 (2018): 1–16, https://doi.org/10.1287/orsc.2017.1172.

6 **employees who are never able:** Laura Huang, Marcia Frideger, and Jone L. Pearce, "Political Skill: Explaining the Effects of Nonnative Accent on Managerial Hiring and Entrepreneurial Investment Decisions," *Journal*

of Applied Psychology 98, no. 6 (2013): 1005–17, https://doi.org/10.1037/a0034125.

6 **medical patients who die:** Brad N. Greenwood, Seth Carnahan, and Laura Huang, "Patient–Physician Gender Concordance and Increased Mortality Among Female Heart Attack Patients," *Proceedings of the National Academy of Sciences* 115, no. 34 (2018): 8569–74, https://doi.org/10.1073/pnas.1800097115.

6 **I've studied how we make perceptions:** Laura Huang and Jone L. Pearce, "Managing the Unknowable: The Effectiveness of Early-Stage Investor Gut Feel in Entrepreneurial Investment Decisions," *Administrative Science Quarterly* 60, no. 4 (2015): 634–70, https://doi.org/10.1177/0001839215597270; Laura Huang and Andrew P. Knight, "Resources and Relationships in Entrepreneurship: An Exchange Theory of the Development and Effects of the Entrepreneur-Investor Relationship," *Academy of Management Review* 42, no. 1 (2015): 80–102, https://doi.org/10.5465/amr.2014.0397; Laura Huang, "The Role of Investor Gut Feel in Managing Complexity and Extreme Risk," *Academy of Management Journal* 61, no. 5 (2018): 1821–47, https://doi.org/10.5465/amj.2016.1009.

CHAPTER 1: HARD WORK, *PLUS*

14 **With this type of work ethic:** Tara Sullivan, "Mirai Nagasu Is a Lesson in Perseverance at Olympics," *Boston Globe*, February 18, 2018, https://www3.bostonglobe.com/sports/2018/02/18/mirai-nagasu-lesson-perseverance-olympics/YmOGUDvMaHtXAT53dmvIZP/story.html?arc404=true; Kimberly Yam, "Mirai Nagasu Says Her Parents' Hard Work in Restaurant Inspires Her Discipline on Ice," *HuffPost* (blog), February 23, 2018, https://www.huffpost.com/entry/mirai-nagasu-credits-her-parents-hard-work-in-restaurant-for-her-own-work-ethic_n_5a8f2a99e4b0ee6416a11a17; Karen Price, "Mirai Nagasu," Team USA, https://www.teamusa.org:443/My-Focus-presented-by-milk-life/Athletes/Mirai-Nagasu.

15 **stories like Gac Filipaj's:** Brenda Schmerl, "Inspirational Stories: How 5 Extraordinary People Beat All Odds to Graduate," *Reader's Digest*, https://www.rd.com/true-stories/inspiring/inspiring-college-graduates.

15 **stories like Sanghoon's:** David Robson, "How Important Is Social Class in Britain Today?" BBC, April 7, 2016, http://www.bbc.com/future/story /20160406-how-much-does-social-class-matter-in-britain-today; David Denby, "Stiff Upper Lips," *New Yorker*, January 20, 2013, https://www .newyorker.com/magazine/2013/01/28/stiff-upper-lips.

16 **Well, before her triumphant:** Dvora Meyers, "The Redemption of Figure Skater Mirai Nagasu," *Deadspin* (blog), January 4, 2018, https://deadspin .com/the-redemption-of-figure-skater-mirai-nagasu-1821763830.

16 **decisions speak louder than denials:** Jeff Yang, "Mirai Nagasu, Ashley Wagner and the Myth of the Golden Girl," *Speakeasy* (blog), *Wall Street Journal*, January 14, 2014, https://blogs.wsj.com/speakeasy/2014/01/14 /mirai-nagasu-ashley-wagner-and-the-myth-of-the-golden-girl.

20 **We are cognitively limited:** C. Neil Macrae and Susanne Quadflieg, "Perceiving People," in *Handbook of Social Psychology*, vol. 1, 5th ed., ed. S. T. Fiske, D. T. Gilbert, and G. Lindzey (Hoboken, NJ: John Wiley & Sons, 2010), 428–63.

20 **Sometimes, our perceptions:** James Dennin, "Ageism and the Reluctance of Companies to Hire Older Workers," Mic, May 9, 2018, https://mic.com /articles/189141/older-workers-are-consistently-discriminated-against -in-job-hiring-heres-how-we-can-fix-that#.8wzxyh5wj.

20 **Research demonstrates that many:** Timothy A. Judge and Daniel M. Cable, "The Effect of Physical Height on Workplace Success and Income: Preliminary Test of a Theoretical Model," *Journal of Applied Psychology* 89, no. 3 (2004): 428–41, https://doi.org/10.1037/0021-9010.89.3.428; M. Dittmann, "Standing Tall Pays Off, Study Finds," *Monitor on Psychology*, July/August 2004; Andreas Schick and Richard H. Steckel, "Height, Human Capital, and Earnings: The Contributions of Cognitive and Noncognitive Ability," *Journal of Human Capital* 9, no. 1 (2015): 94–115, https://doi.org /10.1086/679675; Joe Pinsker, "The Financial Perks of Being Tall," *Atlantic*, May 18, 2015, https://www.theatlantic.com/business/archive/2015/05/the -financial-perks-of-being-tall/393518.

20 **In fact, while only:** Malcolm Gladwell, "The Warren Harding Error: Why We Fall for Tall, Dark, and Handsome Men," in *Blink: The Power of Thinking Without Thinking* (New York: Little, Brown, 2005), 72–98; Vivek Kaul, "The Necktie Syndrome: Why CEOs Tend to Be Significantly

Taller Than the Average Male," *Economic Times*, September 30, 2011, https://economictimes.indiatimes.com/the-necktie-syndrome-why -ceos-tend-to-be-significantly-taller-than-the-average-male/articleshow /10178115.cms.

20 **someone's attractiveness:** Alison Wood Brooks, Laura Huang, Sarah Wood Kearney, and Fiona E. Murray, "Investors Prefer Entrepreneurial Ventures Pitched by Attractive Men," *Proceedings of the National Academy of Sciences* 111, no. 12 (2014): 4427–31, https://doi.org/10.1073/pnas .1321202111.

21 **Disadvantage is situational:** Susanne Quadflieg, Natasha Flannigan, Gordon D. Waiter, Bruno Rossion, Gagan S. Wig, David J. Turk, and C. Neil Macrae, "Stereotype-Based Modulation of Person Perception," *NeuroImage* 57, no. 2 (2011): 549–57, https://doi.org/10.1016/j.neuroimage.2011.05.004.

21 **I've seen males:** Megan Fu, "Male Teachers Claim Wage Discrimination," *Daily Beast*, May 6, 2016, https://www.thedailybeast.com/articles /2016/05/06/male-teachers-claim-wage-discrimination; Bryan G. Nelson, "Dr. Helen Talks About Stereotypes That Male Teachers Face," Men-Teach, April 2, 2009, http://www.menteach.org/news/dr_helen_talks _about_stereotypes_that_male_teachers_face.

22 **blackness is linked to masculinity—but also criminality:** Harry J. Holzer, Steven Raphael, and Michael A. Stoll, "Perceived Criminality, Criminal Background Checks, and the Racial Hiring Practices of Employers," *Journal of Law and Economics* 49, no. 2 (2006): 451–80, https://doi .org/10.1086/501089; Lydia O'Connor, "CNN Analyst Suggests Black People Are 'Prone to Criminality,'" *HuffPost* (blog), July 11, 2016, https:// www.huffpost.com/entry/harry-houck-cnn-blacks-criminality _n_5783f6fae4b01edea78f1434.

22 **older age is connected to trustworthiness:** Helen Dennis and Kathryn Thomas, "Ageism in the Workplace," *Generations* 31, no. 1 (2007), https://www.questia.com/library/journal/1P3-1318281421/ageism-in -the-workplace.

22 **women are perceived to be:** Susan T. Fiske, Amy J. C. Cuddy, and Peter Glick, "Universal Dimensions of Social Cognition: Warmth and Competence," *Trends in Cognitive Sciences* 11, no. 2 (2007): 77–83, https:// doi.org/10.1016/j.tics.2006.11.005; Alice H. Eagly and Steven J. Karau,

"Role Congruity Theory of Prejudice Toward Female Leaders," *Psychological Review* 109, no. 3 (2002): 573–98.

22 **Psychologists Nalini Ambady and Robert Rosenthal:** Nalini Ambady and Robert Rosenthal, "Thin Slices of Expressive Behavior as Predictors of Interpersonal Consequences: A Meta-Analysis," *Psychological Bulletin* 111, no. 2 (1992): 256–74, https://doi.org/10.1037/0033-2909.111.2.256; Nalini Ambady and Robert Rosenthal, "Half a Minute: Predicting Teacher Evaluations from Thin Slices of Nonverbal Behavior and Physical Attractiveness," *Journal of Personality and Social Psychology* 64, no. 3 (1993): 431–41, https://doi.org/10.1037/0022-3514.64.3.431; Nalini Ambady, Frank J. Bernieri, and Jennifer A. Richeson, "Toward a Histology of Social Behavior: Judgmental Accuracy from Thin Slices of the Behavioral Stream," in *Advances in Experimental Social Psychology*, vol. 32, ed. Mark P. Zanna (San Diego: Academic Press, 2000), 201–71, https://doi.org/10.1016/S0065 -2601(00)80006-4.

22 **There's a premium:** Les Picker, "The Growing Importance of Social Skills in the Labor Market," *National Bureau of Economic Research Digest*, November 2015, https://www.nber.org/digest/nov15/w21473 .html.

24 **A branch of psychology:** John T. Jost, Mahzarin R. Banaji, and Brian A. Nosek, "A Decade of System Justification Theory: Accumulated Evidence of Conscious and Unconscious Bolstering of the Status Quo," *Political Psychology* 25, no. 6 (2004): 881–919, https://doi.org/10.1111/j.1467-9221 .2004.00402.x.

24 **Erin Godfrey, a professor:** Melinda D. Anderson, "Why the Myth of Meritocracy Hurts Kids of Color," *Atlantic*, July 27, 2017, https://www .theatlantic.com/education/archive/2017/07/internalizing-the-myth -of-meritocracy/535035/.

24 **Research shows that most successful:** Megan Reitz and John Higgins, "The Problem with Saying 'My Door Is Always Open,'" *Harvard Business Review*, March 9, 2017, https://hbr.org/2017/03/the-problem-with -saying-my-door-is-always-open; John T. Jost and Orsolya Hunyady, "Antecedents and Consequences of System-Justifying Ideologies," *Current Directions in Psychological Science* 14, no. 5 (2005): 260–5, https:// doi.org/10.1111/j.0963-7214.2005.00377.x.

24 **For example, scholars:** David A. Harrison, Kenneth H. Price, and Myrtle P. Bell, "Beyond Relational Demography: Time and the Effects of Surface- and Deep-Level Diversity on Work Group Cohesion," *Academy of Management Journal* 41, no. 1 (1998): 96–107, https://doi.org/10.5465/256901; David A. Harrison, Kenneth H. Price, Joanne H. Gavin, and Anna T. Florey, "Time, Teams, and Task Performance: Changing Effects of Surface- and Deep-Level Diversity on Group Functioning," *Academy of Management Journal* 45, no. 5 (2002): 1029–45, https://doi.org/10.5465/3069328.

24 **Harvard sociologist Letian Zhang:** Letian Zhang, "A Fair Game? Racial Bias and Repeated Interaction Between NBA Coaches and Players," *Administrative Science Quarterly* 62, no. 4 (2017): 603–25, https://doi.org/10.1177/0001839217705375.

24 **researchers such as Freada Kapor Klein and Allison Scott:** Allison Scott, Freada Kapor Klein, Frieda McAlear, Alexis Martin, and Sonia Koshy, *The Leaky Tech Pipeline: A Comprehensive Framework for Understanding and Addressing the Lack of Diversity Across the Tech Ecosystem* (Oakland, CA: Kapor Center for Social Impact, 2018), https://www.kaporcenter.org/the-leaky-tech-pipeline-a-comprehensive-framework-for-understanding-and-addressing-the-lack-of-diversity-across-the-tech-ecosystem/.

25 **"Prejudice doesn't disappear":** Katy Waldman, "A Sociologist Examines the 'White Fragility' That Prevents White Americans from Confronting Racism," *New Yorker*, July 23, 2018, https://www.newyorker.com/books/page-turner/a-sociologist-examines-the-white-fragility-that-prevents-white-americans-from-confronting-racism.

26 **Psychologists Shai Davidai and Thomas Gilovich:** Shai Davidai and Thomas Gilovich, "The Headwinds/Tailwinds Asymmetry: An Availability Bias in Assessments of Barriers and Blessings," *Journal of Personality and Social Psychology* 111, no. 6 (2016): 835–51, https://doi.org/10.1037/pspa0000066.

27 **Nagasu wrote to herself:** Mirai Nagasu (@mirai_nagasu), "Four years ago when I wasn't named to the team, I wrote this poem," Twitter, February 25, 2018, https://twitter.com/mirai_nagasu/status/967815168334774272.

29 **"Everybody makes mistakes":** Scott M. Reid, "After Heartbreak, U.S. Figure Skater Mirai Nagasu Again Takes Aim at Olympic Bid," *Orange*

County Register, January 2, 2018, https://www.ocregister.com/2018/01
/02/after-heartbreak-u-s-figure-skater-mirai-nagasu-again-takes-aim
-at-olympic-bid.

CHAPTER 2: YOUR BASIC GOODS

34 **Why didn't Poincaré:** Sreeraj Thekkeyil, "Which Scientists Deserved to
Win a Nobel Prize but Never Won?" Quora, May 18, 2018, https://www
.quora.com/Which-scientists-deserved-to-win-a-Nobel-Prize-but
-never-won.

38 **Captivated, I spent:** "Made in Texas: The Buc-ee's Success Story," *Texas
Monthly*, February 26, 2013, https://www.texasmonthly.com/articles/made
-in-texas-the-buc-ees-success-story/.

38 **"What's not great about Buc-ee's":** Gemma Nisbet, "Beavers Are Better
at the World's Biggest Service Station," West Travel Club, July 23, 2017,
https://westtravelclub.com.au/stories/biggest-is-better-at-texas-adult
-amusement-park.

41 **Warren Buffett, American businessman:** Farnam Street, "The 'Circle
of Competence' Theory Will Help You Make Vastly Smarter Decisions,"
Business Insider, December 5, 2013, https://www.businessinsider.com/the
-circle-of-competence-theory-2013-12; Fred Nickols and Harvey Berg-
holz, "The Consultant's Competency Circle: A Tool for Gauging Your
Success Potential as an Independent Consultant," *Performance Improvement* 52, no. 2 (2013): 37–41, https://doi.org/10.1002/pfi.21328.

41 **Buffett once described:** Farnam Street, "Understanding Your Circle of
Competence: How Warren Buffett Avoids Problems," *Farnam Street*
(blog), December 1, 2013, https://fs.blog/2013/12/circle-of-competence/.

42 **Charlie Munger, Warren Buffett's right-hand man:** Tren Griffin,
"Charlie Munger on 'Circle of Competence' (the Second Essential Filter),"
25iq (blog), December 22, 2012, https://25iq.com/2012/12/22/charlie
-munger-on-circle-of-competence-the-second-essential-filter.

43 **Billionaire entrepreneur Richard Branson:** Natalie Clarkson, "Why
Did Richard Branson Start an Airline?" Virgin, October 1, 2014, https://
www.virgin.com/travel/why-did-richard-branson-start-airline.

44 **One version of the story:** Ibid.

44 **a company whose signature:** Glen Sanford, "iPhone," Apple-History, https://apple-history.com/iphone; "iPhone History: A Timeline from 2007–2019," History Cooperative, September 14, 2014, https://history cooperative.org/the-history-of-the-iphone.

CHAPTER 3: RECOGNITION OF THE INCONGRUOUS

51 **Turns out, the husband:** Mr. Li, interviews with author, Din Tai Fung, Taiwan, August 18, 2017, and July 22, 2018.

52 **We tend to look:** Benigno E. Aguirre, Dennis Wenger, and Gabriela Vigo, "A Test of the Emergent Norm Theory of Collective Behavior," *Sociological Forum* 13, no. 2 (1998): 301–20, https://link.springer.com /article/10.1023/A:1022145900928.

52 **This type of herd mentality:** Ha V. Dang and Mi Lin, "Herd Mentality in the Stock Market: On the Role of Idiosyncratic Participants with Heterogeneous Information," *International Review of Financial Analysis* 48 (2016): 247–60, https://doi.org/10.1016/j.irfa.2016.10.005; Scott Cooley, "Technology and the Herd Mentality," *Mortgage Banking* 64, no. 9 (2004): 122–4.

52 **In my research:** Huang, "The Role of Investor Gut Feel in Managing Complexity and Extreme Risk"; Laura Huang, Andy Wu, Min Ju Lee, Jiayi Bao, Marianne Hudson, and Elaine Bolle, *The American Angel: The First In-depth Report on the Demographics and Investing Activity of Individual American Angel Investors* (Wharton Entrepreneurship and Angel Capital Association, November 2017), https://www.angelcapitalassociation .org/data/Documents/TAAReport11-30-17.pdf?rev=DB68; Laura Huang, "A Theory of Investor Gut Feel: A Test of the Impact of Gut Feel on Entrepreneurial Investment Decisions" (PhD diss., University of California, Irvine, 2012).

53 **By 1986, we saw:** Mary Bellis, "History of the IBM PC," ThoughtCo, May 12, 2019, https://www.thoughtco.com/history-of-the-ibm-pc-1991408.

55 **Priced at around three hundred dollars:** "Asus Company History," *Gadget Reviews* (blog), http://mylaptopyourlaptop.blogspot.com/2012/04 /asus-company-history.html; Dan Ackerman, "The Asus Eee PC Family Tree," *CNET*, February 17, 2010, https://www.cnet.com/news/the-asus -eee-pc-family-tree; JerryJ, "Asus Reveals Pricing for the Eee PC Mini

Laptop," *Brighthand* (blog), October 18, 2007, http://www.brighthand .com/news/asus-reveals-pricing-for-the-eee-pc-mini-laptop/.

55 **Asus continues to manufacture:** Evan Comen, "Check Out How Much a Computer Cost the Year You Were Born," *USA Today*, June 22, 2018, https://www.usatoday.com/story/tech/2018/06/22/cost-of-a-computer -the-year-you-were-born/36156373/; Andrew, "Most Popular Laptops for May 2007," *Notebook Review* (blog), June 4, 2007, http://www.notebook review.com/news/most-popular-laptops-for-may-2007/; Jon Turi, "Gadget Rewind 2007: ASUS Eee PC 4G," *Engadget* (blog), June 1, 2014, https:// www.engadget.com/2014/06/01/gadget-rewind-2007-asus-eee-pc-4g.

56 **The brilliant management:** Ryan Raffaelli, "Technology Reemergence: Creating New Value for Old Technologies in Swiss Mechanical Watch- making, 1970–2008," *Administrative Science Quarterly* (2018), 00018392 18778505, https://doi.org/10.1177/0001839218778505.

56 **Global Swiss watch:** Joe Thompson, "For Swiss Watches, America Is Back," *Bloomberg*, July 25, 2018, https://www.bloomberg.com/news /articles/2018-07-25/the-swiss-luxury-watch-slump-in-the-united -states-is-over.

62 **"Not all juice is equal":** Derek Thompson, "How Juicero's Story Set the Company Up for Humiliation," *Atlantic*, April 21, 2017, https://www .theatlantic.com/business/archive/2017/04/juicero-lessons/523896/.

CHAPTER 4: THE VALUE OF CONSTRAINTS

69 **I suspect that the constraint:** David R. Francis, "Employers' Replies to Racial Names," National Bureau of Economic Research Digest, Sep- tember 2003, https://www.nber.org/digest/sep03/w9873.html; Alexia Elejalde-Ruiz, "Hiring Bias Study: Resumes with Black, White, Hispanic Names Treated the Same," *Chicago Tribune*, May 4, 2016, https://www .chicagotribune.com/business/ct-bias-hiring-0504-biz-20160503-story .html; Dina Gerdeman, "Minorities Who 'Whiten' Job Resumes Get More Interviews," HBS Working Knowledge, May 17, 2017, http://hbswk.hbs .edu/item/minorities-who-whiten-job-resumes-get-more-interviews; Sonia K. Kang, Katherine A. DeCelles, András Tilcsik, and Sora Jun, "Whitened Résumés: Race and Self-Presentation in the Labor Market,"

Administrative Science Quarterly 61, no. 3 (2016): 469–502, https://doi
.org/10.1177/0001839216639577.

71 **We have a tendency:** Daniel Kahneman and Amos Tversky, "Prospect
Theory: An Analysis of Decision Under Risk," in *Handbook of the Fundamentals of Financial Decision Making: Part 1*, ed. Leonard C. MacLean
and William T. Ziemba, World Scientific Handbook in Financial Economics Series (Singapore: World Scientific, 2013), 99–127, https://doi.org/10.1142
/9789814417358_0006.

71 **Arlan Hamilton, a venture capitalist:** Arlan Hamilton, personal communication with author, Backstage Capital Crew Meeting, Los Angeles,
April 17, 2018.

73 **This is backed by:** Tara Sophia Mohr, "Why Women Don't Apply for
Jobs Unless They're 100% Qualified," *Harvard Business Review*, August
25, 2014, https://hbr.org/2014/08/why-women-dont-apply-for-jobs-unless
-theyre-100-qualified.

74 **A team of clever researchers:** Markus Baer, Kurt T. Dirks, and Jackson
A. Nickerson, "Microfoundations of Strategic Problem Formulation,"
Strategic Management Journal 34, no. 2 (2013): 197–214, https://doi.org
/10.1002/smj.2004.

75 **By reframing the problem:** "Audi with Most Fuel-Efficient Powertrain
at Le Mans," Motorsport.com, June 9, 2014, https://www.motorsport.com
/lemans/news/audi-with-most-fuel-efficient-powertrain-at-le-mans
/452641/.

77 **The executives behind:** Joerg Schreiner, "Corporate Incubators: The
Good, the Bad and the Ugly," *Co-Shift* (blog), September 7, 2017, https://
www.co-shift.com/why-corporate-incubators-fail-at-innovation-transfer/.

77 **Good ideas and good intentions:** Amr Kebbi and Dave Valliere, "The
Double J-Curve: A Model for Incubated Start-ups" (11th European
Conference on Innovation and Entrepreneurship, Jyvaskyla, Finland,
2016), 371–80, https://www.researchgate.net/publication/309033445
_The_Double_J-Curve_A_Model_for_Incubated_Start-ups; Cliff Oxford,
"Trouble in Paradise: Why Business Incubators Don't Work," *Forbes*, June
30, 2014, https://www.forbes.com/sites/cliffoxford/2014/06/30/trouble-in
-paradise-why-business-incubators-dont-work/#60b0dc164d87; Bridge for
Billions, "3 Problems with Traditional Incubators and Accelerators,"

Medium, July 31, 2016, https://medium.com/bridgeforbillions/3-problems
-with-traditional-incubators-and-accelerators-a29354e30564.

78 **They don't face:** Joao Sousa, Raquel Meneses, Humberto Ribeiro, and
Sandra Raquel Alves, "The Symbiotic Relationship Between Startups and
Incubators," in *Economic and Social Development: Book of Proceedings*,
ed. Rozana Veselica, Gordana Dukic, and Khalid Hammes, International
Scientific Conference on Economic and Social Development (Zagreb,
Croatia: Varazdin Development and Entrepreneurship Agency, 2018),
823–34, http://www.esd-conference.com/upload/book_of_proceedings
/Book_of_Proceedings_esdZagreb2018_Online.pdf.

CHAPTER 5: HONING YOUR GUT FEEL
AND WHAT YOU BRING TO THE TABLE

82 **Kristie Paskvan:** Melissa Jeltsen, "Illinois Will Teach Hairdressers to
Recognize Victims of Domestic Violence," *HuffPost* (blog), December 1,
2016, https://www.huffpost.com/entry/illinois-will-teach-hairdressers-to
-recognize-signs-of-domestic-violence_n_583f2717e4b09e21702c3122.

84 **rather than subconscious:** Gladwell, *Blink*, 10.

84 **But when we need to make decisions:** Gerd Gigerenzer, *Gut Feelings:
The Intelligence of the Unconscious* (New York: Penguin Books, 2008).

84 **To illustrate: I found:** Huang and Pearce, "Managing the Unknowable."

85 **but you're going:** Peter Cappelli, "Your Approach to Hiring Is All
Wrong," *Harvard Business Review*, May–June 2019, https://hbr.org/2019
/05/recruiting; Boris Groysberg, Nitin Nohria, and Claudio Fernández-
Aráoz, "The Definitive Guide to Recruiting in Good Times and Bad," *Harvard Business Review*, May 2009, https://hbr.org/2009/05/the-definitive
-guide-to-recruiting-in-good-times-and-bad.

85 **Management scholars Robert Costigan and Kyle Brink:** Robert D.
Costigan and Kyle E. Brink, "On the Prevalence of Linear versus Nonlinear Thinking in Undergraduate Business Education: A Lot of Rhetoric,
Not Enough Evidence," *Journal of Management & Organization* 21, no. 4
(2015): 535–47, https://doi.org/10.1017/jmo.2014.86; Bart de Langhe, Ste-
fano Puntoni, and Richard Larrick, "Linear Thinking in a Nonlinear
World," *Harvard Business Review*, May–June 2017, https://hbr.org/2017

/05/linear-thinking-in-a-nonlinear-world; Mark Bonchek, "How to Create an Exponential Mindset," *Harvard Business Review*, July 27, 2016,
https://hbr.org/2016/07/how-to-create-an-exponential-mindset.

85 **In 1946, a woman:** "The History of Diapers—Disposable & Cloth The
History of Diapers," Diaper Jungle, October 1, 2016, https://www.diaper
jungle.com/pages/history-of-diapers; Sarah Laskow, "The Woman Who
Invented Disposable Diapers," *Atlantic*, October 14, 2014, https://www
.theatlantic.com/technology/archive/2014/10/the-woman-who
-invented-disposable-diapers/381310.

87 **It's taking what you have:** Goethe University Frankfurt, "Smart People Have Better Connected Brains," *ScienceDaily*, November 22, 2017,
https://www.sciencedaily.com/releases/2017/11/171122103552.htm.

87 **Companies that can do it:** Ted Baker and Reed E. Nelson, "Creating
Something from Nothing: Resource Construction Through Entrepreneurial Bricolage," *Administrative Science Quarterly* 50, no. 3 (2005):
329–66, https://doi.org/10.2189/asqu.2005.50.3.329.

96 **"luxury, not a necessity":** Sarah Gordon, "Ryanair Confirms It WILL
Bring in Charges for Use of On-board Toilets," *Daily Mail*, April 6, 2010,
https://www.dailymail.co.uk/travel/article-1263905/Ryanair-toilet
-charges-phased-in.html; "Stephen McNamara, spokesperson for the
airline, told TravelMail: 'By charging for the toilets we are hoping to
change passenger behaviour so that they use the bathroom before or after
the flight.'"

96 **I also heard:** Tim Clark, "Ryanair Announce Plans to Launch 'Vertical
Seats' from Just £4," *Daily Mail*, July 2, 2010, https://www.dailymail.co.uk
/travel/article-1291131/Ryanair-launch-vertical-seating-Standing-room
-tickets-4.html.

96 **Ryanair encourages those articles:** George Hobica, president of air
farewatchdog.com, said Ryanair is doing this mostly for publicity: "Their
CEO loves to get his picture on TV" (Scott Mayerowitz, "Paying to Pee:
Have the Airlines Gone Too Far?" ABC News, April 13, 2010, https://
abcnews.go.com/Travel/Green/paying-pee-airlines-critics-call
-ryanairs-fee-inhumane/story?id=10355139).

99 **In fact, people find it so psychologically stressful:** Leon Festinger,
A Theory of Cognitive Dissonance (Stanford, CA: Stanford University

Press, 1957); Elliot Aronson, "The Theory of Cognitive Dissonance: A Current Perspective," in *Advances in Experimental Social Psychology*, vol. 4, ed. Leonard Berkowitz (New York: Academic Press, 1969), 1–34, https://doi.org/10.1016/S0065-2601(08)60075-1.

CHAPTER 6: THE POWER OF THE UNEXPECTED

106 **I recently asked Hasan Minhaj:** Hasan Minhaj, conversation with author and Preet Bharara, Cafe Change Summit, New York, April 26, 2018.

106 **Psychologists Brad Bitterly:** T. Bradford Bitterly, Alison Wood Brooks, and Maurice E. Schweitzer, "Risky Business: When Humor Increases and Decreases Status," *Journal of Personality and Social Psychology* 112, no. 3 (2017): 431–55, https://doi.org/10.1037/pspi0000079.

107 **Benign violation theory:** A. Peter McGraw and Caleb Warren, "Benign Violation Theory," in *Encyclopedia of Humor Studies*, ed. Salvatore Attardo (Thousand Oaks, CA: Sage Publications, 2014), 75–7; Caleb Warren and A. Peter McGraw, "Opinion: What Makes Things Humorous," *Proceedings of the National Academy of Sciences of the United States of America* 112, no. 23 (2015): 7105–6, https://doi.org/10.1073/pnas.1503836112.

108 **Delight unsettles and challenges:** Joëlle Vanhamme, "The Surprise-Delight Relationship Revisited in the Management of Experience," *Recherche et Applications en Marketing (English Edition)* 23, no. 3 (2008): 113–38, https://doi.org/10.1177/205157070802300307; Soma Dey, Sanjukta Ghosh, Biplab Datta, and Parama Barai, "A Study on the Antecedents and Consequences of Customer Delight," *Total Quality Management & Business Excellence* 28, nos. 1–2 (2017): 47–61, https://doi.org/10.1080/14783363.2015.1049146; Vincent P. Magnini, John C. Crotts, and Anita Zehrer, "Understanding Customer Delight: An Application of Travel Blog Analysis," *Journal of Travel Research* 50, no. 5 (2011): 535–45, https://doi.org/10.1177/0047287510379162.

109 **Production of a movie:** Nicole Sperling, "How *Crazy Rich Asians* Gave Director Jon M. Chu a Voice," *Vanity Fair*, August 10, 2018, https://www.vanityfair.com/hollywood/2018/08/crazy-rich-asians-director-jon-m-chu.

109 **headed by Singapore chef:** Alyse Whitney, "Dumplings, Kaya Toast, and Chili Crab: Inside the Food of *Crazy Rich Asians*," *Bon Appétit*, August 30, 2018, https://www.bonappetit.com/story/crazy-rich-asians-food-singapore; Kenneth Goh, "Behind the Food in 'Crazy Rich Asians,'" Michelin Guide, August 22, 2018, https://guide.michelin.com/us/en/illinois/chicago/article/features/crazy-rich-asians-movie-food-styling.

109 **"that crazy blend of identities and cultures":** Shannon Connellan, "Read the Beautiful Letter That Allowed 'Crazy Rich Asians' to Use Coldplay's 'Yellow,'" Mashable, August 19, 2018, https://mashable.com/article/crazy-rich-asians-coldplay.

110 **Chu wanted to use the song:** Kat Chow, "If We Called Ourselves Yellow," NPR, September 27, 2018, https://www.npr.org/sections/codeswitch/2018/09/27/647989652/if-we-called-ourselves-yellow.

110 **Instead he wrote:** World Entertainment News Network, "Coldplay Almost Didn't Let 'Crazy Rich Asians' Use 'Yellow' Due to Racism Fears," Canoe.com, August 16, 2018, https://canoe.com/entertainment/music/coldplay-almost-didnt-let-crazy-rich-asians-use-yellow-due-to-racism-fears.

112 **They later watched:** Julia Emmanuele, "All the Songs in 'Crazy Rich Asians' That You'll Want to Listen to Over & Over Again," *Bustle*, August 25, 2018, https://www.bustle.com/p/all-the-songs-in-crazy-rich-asians-that-youll-want-to-listen-to-over-over-again-10239631.

112 **The value this provided:** Laurent Bach, Patrick Cohendet, Julien Pénin, and Laurent Simon, "Creative Industries and the IPR Dilemma Between Appropriation and Creation: Some Insights from the Videogame and Music Industries," *Management International* 14, no. 3 (2010): 59–72, https://doi.org/10.7202/044293ar.

CHAPTER 7: REFLECTIVE IMPROVISATION

117 **The company manufactured:** Susan Levine, "He Sees Fortune in Chicken Contact Lens," *Chicago Tribune*, November 23, 1989, https://www.chicagotribune.com/news/ct-xpm-1989-11-23-8903120133-story

.html; Bruce G. Posner, "Seeing Red," *Inc.*, May 1, 1989, https://www.inc
.com/magazine/19890501/5636.html.

119 **As Napoléon Bonaparte:** "Napoleon Bonaparte: Over-Preparation Is
the Foe of Inspiration," AZ Quotes, https://www.azquotes.com/quote
/1056571.

119 **Martin Seligman's:** Martin E. Seligman, "On the Generality of the Laws
of Learning," *Psychological Review* 77, no. 5 (1970): 406–18, https://doi
.org/10.1037/h0029790.

119 **It can lull people:** J. H. Mandel, E. C. Rich, M. G. Luxenberg, M. T.
Spilane, D. C. Kern, and T. A. Parrino, "Preparation for Practice in Inter-
nal Medicine: A Study of Ten Years of Residency Graduates," *Archives of
Internal Medicine* 148, no. 4 (1988): 853–56; Kazuya Nakayachi, Branden
B. Johnson, and Kazuki Koketsu, "Effects of Acknowledging Uncertainty
About Earthquake Risk Estimates on San Francisco Bay Area Residents'
Beliefs, Attitudes, and Intentions," *Risk Analysis* 38, no. 4 (2018): 666–79,
https://doi.org/10.1111/risa.12883.

CHAPTER 8: SHAPING AND DELIGHTING IN SITU

129 **It's what landed Sara Blakely:** Guy Raz, "How a Pitch in a Neiman
Marcus Ladies Room Changed Sara Blakely's Life," NPR, September 12,
2016, https://www.npr.org/templates/transcript/transcript.php?storyId=
493312213.

136 **In research I've conducted:** Francesca Gino, Ovul Sezer, and Laura
Huang, "To Be or Not to Be Your Authentic Self? Catering to Others'
Preferences Hinders Performance" (working paper, Harvard Business
School, 2016).

140 **Aileen Lee, venture capital investor:** Aileen Lee, phone conversation
with author, July 17, 2017.

140 **Incidentally, she is:** Aileen Lee, "Welcome to the Unicorn Club: Learning from Billion-Dollar Startups," *TechCrunch* (blog), 2013, http://social
.techcrunch.com/2013/11/02/welcome-to-the-unicorn-club/.

CHAPTER 9: ALL THE WAYS YOUR DIAMOND SPARKLES

149 **As far back as 1890:** William James, "The Perception of Reality," in *The Principles of Psychology*, vol. 2 (New York: Henry Holt and Company, 1890), 283–324.

149 **As researchers gained more clarity:** Gordon W. Allport, "The Ego in Contemporary Psychology," *Psychological Review* 50, no. 5 (1943): 451–78, https://doi.org/10.1037/h0055375; Shelley Duval and Robert A. Wicklund, *A Theory of Objective Self Awareness* (San Diego: Academic Press, 1972); Paul J. Silvia and T. Shelley Duval, "Objective Self-Awareness Theory: Recent Progress and Enduring Problems," *Personality and Social Psychology Review* 5, no. 3 (2001): 230–41, https://doi.org/10.1207/S15327957 PSPR0503_4; Robert A. Wicklund, "Objective Self-Awareness," in *Advances in Experimental Social Psychology*, vol. 8, ed. Leonard Berkowitz (San Diego: Academic Press, 1975), 233–75, http://www.sciencedirect.com /science/article/pii/S006526010860252X.

150 **Science has its own version:** Isabel Briggs Myers, Mary H. McCaulley, Naomi L. Quenk, and Allen L. Hammer, *MBTI Manual: A Guide to the Development and Use of the Myers-Briggs Type Indicator*, 3rd ed. (Palo Alto, CA: Consulting Psychologists Press, 2003).

150 **In fact, tests like the MBTI:** Robert R. McCrae and Paul T. Costa, "Reinterpreting the Myers-Briggs Type Indicator from the Perspective of the Five-Factor Model of Personality," *Journal of Personality* 57, no. 1 (1989): 17–40.

150 **We use tests like the MBTI:** John M. Digman, "Personality Structure: Emergence of the Five-Factor Model," *Annual Review of Psychology* 41, no. 1 (1990): 417–40, https://doi.org/10.1146/annurev.ps.41.020190.002221; Boele De Raad, *The Big Five Personality Factors: The Psycholexical Approach to Personality* (Ashland, OH: Hogrefe & Huber, 2000); Jerry S. Wiggins, ed., *The Five-Factor Model of Personality: Theoretical Perspectives* (New York: Guilford Press, 1996); John A. Johnson, "Clarification of Factor Five with the Help of the AB5C Model," *European Journal of Personality* 8, no. 4 (1994): 311–34, https://doi.org/10.1002/per.2410080408; Colin G. DeYoung, Lena C. Quilty, and Jordan B. Peterson, "Between

Facets and Domains: 10 Aspects of the Big Five," *Journal of Personality and Social Psychology* 93, no. 5 (2007): 880–96, https://doi.org/10.1037/0022-3514.93.5.880; Colin G. DeYoung, Bridget E. Carey, Robert F. Krueger, and Scott R. Ross, "Ten Aspects of the Big Five in the Personality Inventory for *DSM-5*," *Personality Disorders* 7, no. 2 (2016): 113–23, https://doi.org/10.1037/per0000170; Michael C. Ashton, Kibeom Lee, Lewis R. Goldberg, and Reinout E. de Vries, "Higher Order Factors of Personality: Do They Exist?" *Personality and Social Psychology Review* 13, no. 2 (2009): 79–91, https://doi.org/10.1177/1088868309338467.

151 **"be a first-rate version":** Judy Garland, "Judy Garland Quotes," BrainyQuote, https://www.brainyquote.com/quotes/judy_garland_104276.

153 **Instead, we have the power:** D. Scott DeRue, Susan J. Ashford, and Natalie C. Cotton, "Assuming the Mantle: Unpacking the Process by Which Individuals Internalize a Leader Identity," in *Exploring Positive Identities and Organizations: Building a Theoretical and Research Foundation*, ed. Laura Morgan Roberts and Jane E. Dutton, Organization and Management Series (New York: Psychology Press, 2009).

153 **She cofounded a tech nonprofit:** Ashley Edwards, conversations with author, April 26, 2018, and May 16, 2018.

157 **Ashley realized that by embracing:** Allen R. McConnell, "The Multiple Self-Aspects Framework: Self-Concept Representation and Its Implications," *Personality and Social Psychology Review* 15, no. 1 (2011): 3–27, https://doi.org/10.1177/1088868310371101.

157 **Self-awareness, in fact:** David M. Buss and Michael F. Scheier, "Self-Consciousness, Self-Awareness, and Self-Attribution," *Journal of Research in Personality* 10, no. 4 (1976): 463–68, https://doi.org/10.1016/0092-6566(76)90060-X; Fred Rothbaum, John R. Weisz, and Samuel S. Snyder, "Changing the World and Changing the Self: A Two-Process Model of Perceived Control," *Journal of Personality and Social Psychology* 42, no. 1 (1982): 5–37.

157 **As William James wrote:** William James, *The Principles of Psychology*, vol. 1 (New York: Henry Holt and Company, 1890), 294.

157 **We come to know ourselves:** Herbert Blumer, *Symbolic Interactionism: Perspective and Method* (Berkeley, CA: University of California Press, 1986); Joel M. Charon, *Symbolic Interactionism: An Introduction, an*

Interpretation, an Integration (Englewood Cliffs, NJ: Prentice-Hall, 1979), https://trove.nla.gov.au/version/45014982.

158 **A few months after:** Ashton Kutcher, conversation with author, Wharton Social Impact Initiative's Lauren and Bobby Turner Social Impact Executive Speaker Series, Philadelphia, October 10, 2013.

CHAPTER 10: TURNING BIASES AND STEREOTYPES IN YOUR FAVOR

168 **Classic research on social perception:** Mark Snyder, Elizabeth Decker Tanke, and Ellen Berscheid, "Social Perception and Interpersonal Behavior: On the Self-fulfilling Nature of Social Stereotypes," *Journal of Personality and Social Psychology* 35, no. 9 (1977): 656–66, http://dx.doi.org /10.1037/0022-3514.35.9.656; Penelope J. Oakes, S. Alexander Haslam, and John C. Turner, *Stereotyping and Social Reality* (Oxford, UK: Blackwell, 1994).

168 **Psychologists Mahzarin Banaji and Brian Nosek:** Irene V. Blair and Mahzarin R. Banaji, "Automatic and Controlled Processes in Stereotype Priming," *Journal of Personality and Social Psychology* 70, no. 6 (1996): 1142–63, https://doi.org/10.1037/0022-3514.70.6.1142; Anthony G. Greenwald, Mahzarin R. Banaji, and Brian A. Nosek, "Statistically Small Effects of the Implicit Association Test Can Have Societally Large Effects," *Journal of Personality and Social Psychology* 108, no. 4 (2015): 553–61, https:// doi.org/10.1037/pspa0000016.

172 **"I ask them if they have":** Cyrus Habib, interview with moderators, Cafe Change Summit, New York, April 26, 2018.

173 **"I take the opportunity to walk with them":** Ibid.

173 **And that has allowed Cyrus:** Mike Baker, "Life Story Drives Blind Lawmaker," *Seattle Times*, March 10, 2013, https://www.seattletimes.com /seattle-news/life-story-drives-blind-lawmaker/.

173 **Paul Graham:** Alyson Shontell, "Startup Titan Paul Graham Explains Why He Said Founders with Thick Accents Get Worse Results," *Business Insider*, August 27, 2013, https://www.businessinsider.com/paul-graham -on-startup-founders-with-thick-foreign-accents-2013-8.

174 **And it just so happened:** Huang, Frideger, and Pearce, "Political Skill."

175 **When bias is confronted:** Elizabeth S. Focella, Meghan G. Bean, and Jeff Stone, "Confrontation and Beyond: Examining a Stigmatized Target's Use of a Prejudice Reduction Strategy," *Social & Personality Psychology Compass* 9, no. 2 (2015): 100–14, https://doi.org/10.1111/spc3.12153; Patricia G. Devine, "Stereotypes and Prejudice: Their Automatic and Controlled Components," *Journal of Personality and Social Psychology* 56, no. 1 (1989): 5–18, https://doi.org/10.1037/0022-3514.56.1.5; James L. Hilton and William von Hippel, "Stereotypes," *Annual Review of Psychology* 47, no. 1 (1996): 237–71, https://doi.org/10.1146/annurev.psych.47.1.237; Crystal Fleming, Michèle Lamont, and Jessica Welburn, "African Americans Respond to Stigmatization: The Meanings and Salience of Confronting, Deflecting Conflict, Educating the Ignorant and 'Managing the Self,'" *Ethnic and Racial Studies* 35, no. 3 (2012): 400–17.

176 **Psychologists Alexander Czopp:** Alexander M. Czopp, Margo J. Monteith, and Aimee Y. Mark, "Standing Up for a Change: Reducing Bias Through Interpersonal Confrontation," *Journal of Personality & Social Psychology* 90, no. 5 (2006): 784–803, https://doi.org/10.1037/0022-3514.90.5.784.

176 **Recognize and adapt:** John Szramiak, "Here's a 10 Point Plan to Invest like Charlie Munger," *Business Insider*, October 26, 2016, https://www.businessinsider.com/10-point-plan-to-invest-like-charlie-munger-2016-10.

176 **When Dawn Fitzpatrick:** Alexandra Stevenson and Kate Kelly, "Men Bet She Would Fail; Now She Runs a $26 Billion Fund," *New York Times*, April 8, 2017, https://www.nytimes.com/2017/04/08/business/dealbook/george-soros-dawn-fitzpatrick-american-stock-exchange.html; Dawn Fitzpatrick, interview by S. Ruhle and M. Miller, *Bloomberg Television*, June 26, 2014; Julie Segal, "Dawn Fitzpatrick Leaves UBS for Soros CIO Job," *Institutional Investor*, February 1, 2017, https://www.institutionalinvestor.com/article/b1505q22yk2j2m/dawn-fitzpatrick-leaves-ubs-for-soros-cio-job.

177 **there are single moments in time:** Ibid.

177 **In my research and in the research:** David Willer, Michael J. Lovaglia, and Barry Markovsky, "Power and Influence: A Theoretical Bridge," *Social Forces* 76, no. 2 (1997): 571–603, https://doi.org/10.1093/sf/76.2.571; Linda L. Carli, "Gender, Interpersonal Power, and Social Influence," *Journal of*

Social Issues 55, no. 1 (1999): 81–99, https://doi.org/10.1111/0022-4537.00106; Huang and Knight, "Resources and Relationships in Entrepreneurship."

177 **It's not a bad thing:** Steven L. Blader and Ya-Ru Chen, "Differentiating the Effects of Status and Power: A Justice Perspective," *Journal of Personality and Social Psychology* 102, no. 5 (2012): 994–1014, https://doi.org/10.1037/a0026651.

178 **Cooperative interdependence and competitive interdependence:** Harold H. Kelley and John W. Thibaut, *Interpersonal Relations: A Theory of Interdependence* (New York: John Wiley & Sons, 1978).

CHAPTER 11: FRAMING PERCEPTIONS AND ATTRIBUTIONS *YOUR* WAY

184 **I've found that entrepreneurs:** Huang, "A Theory of Investor Gut Feel."

185 **For example, Melissa Cardon:** Melissa S. Cardon, Joakim Wincent, Jagdip Singh, and Mateja Drnovsek, "The Nature and Experience of Entrepreneurial Passion," *Academy of Management Review* 34, no. 3 (2009): 511–32, https://doi.org/10.5465/AMR.2009.40633190.

185 **The influence of such passion:** Xiao-Ping Chen, Xin Yao, and Suresh Kotha, "Entrepreneur Passion and Preparedness in Business Plan Presentations: A Persuasion Analysis of Venture Capitalists' Funding Decisions," *Academy of Management Journal* 52, no. 1 (2009): 199–214, https://doi.org/10.5465/amj.2009.36462018; Robert A. Baron, "The Role of Affect in the Entrepreneurial Process," *Academy of Management Review* 33, no. 2 (2008): 328–40; Antonio Damasio, "Feelings of Emotion and the Self," *Annals of the New York Academy of Sciences* 1001, no. 1 (2003): 253–61, https://doi.org/10.1196/annals.1279.014; Norbert Schwarz and Gerald L. Clore, "Mood as Information: 20 Years Later," *Psychological Inquiry* 14, nos. 3–4 (2003): 296–303, https://doi.org/10.1080/1047840X.2003.9682896.

186 **This type of "spotlight effect":** Thomas Gilovich, Victoria Husted Medvec, and Kenneth Savitsky, "The Spotlight Effect in Social Judgment: An Egocentric Bias in Estimates of the Salience of One's Own Actions and Appearance," *Journal of Personality and Social Psychology* 78, no. 2 (2000): 211–22; Thomas Gilovich and Kenneth Savitsky, "The Spotlight Effect and the Illusion of Transparency: Egocentric Assessments of How

We Are Seen by Others," *Current Directions in Psychological Science* 8, no. 6 (1999): 165–68, https://doi.org/10.1111/1467-8721.00039; Thomas Gilovich, Justin Kruger, and Victoria Husted Medvec, "The Spotlight Effect Revisited: Overestimating the Manifest Variability of Our Actions and Appearance," *Journal of Experimental Social Psychology* 38, no. 1 (2002): 93–99, https://doi.org/10.1006/jesp.2001.1490.

191 **women in mathematics:** Hannah-Hanh Nguyen and Ann Marie Ryan, "Does Stereotype Threat Affect Test Performance of Minorities and Women? A Meta-Analysis of Experimental Evidence," *Journal of Applied Psychology* 93, no. 6 (2008): 1314–34, http://dx.doi.org/10.1037/a0012702.

CHAPTER 12: YOU NEED AT LEAST TWO POINTS TO CREATE A TRAJECTORY

195 **The trajectory of an academic:** Barry Yeoman, "Academic Apprentices: Still an Ideal?" *Barry Yeoman: Journalist* (blog), May 1, 1999, https://barryyeoman.com/1999/05/academic-apprentices-still-an-ideal/; Karen Forbes, "The PhD Experience as an Apprenticeship into Academia," *FERSA University of Cambridge Blog*, March 9, 2018, https://fersacambridge.com/2018/03/09/the-phd-experience-as-an-apprenticeship-into-academia.

202 **Many different trajectories:** Daniel Bertaux and Martin Kohli, "The Life Story Approach: A Continental View," *Annual Review of Sociology* 10, no. 1 (1984): 215–37, https://doi.org/10.1146/annurev.so.10.080184.001243; Stephanie Taylor and Karen Littleton, "Biographies in Talk: A Narrative-Discursive Research Approach," *Qualitative Sociology Review* 2, no. 1 (2006): 22–38.

206 **The world can be cruel:** Dave Dahl, conversation with author, ENIAC VC M1 Summit, San Francisco, November 15, 2016.

207 **Remember that 75 percent:** Lolly Daskal, "How to Be More Resilient When Things Get Tough," *Inc.*, April 9, 2015, https://www.inc.com/lolly-daskal/how-to-be-more-resilient-when-things-get-tough.html.

INDEX